6502 Machine Code for Beginners

A. P. Stephenson

Newnes Technical Books

Newnes Technical Books
is an imprint of the Butterworth Group
which has principal offices in
London, Boston, Durban, Singapore, Sydney, Toronto, Wellington

First published 1983
  Reprinted 1983

© **Butterworth & Co. (Publishers) Ltd, 1983**
  Borough Green, Sevenoaks, Kent TN15 8PH, England

British Library Cataloguing in Publication Data

Stephenson, A. P.
  6502 machine code for beginners.
  1. MOS Technology Inc. 6502 (Computer)
  2. Assembler language (Computer program language)
  I. Title
  001.64'24   QA76.8.M67

ISBN 0-408-01311-7

Filmset by Tunbridge Wells Typesetting Services Ltd
Printed in England by Page Bros (Norwich) Ltd.

Preface

The steep fall in price and the increase in power of the microcomputer has caused an explosion of interest in home computing. In the UK, the launching of the BBC microcomputer together with the excellent TV programmes will inevitably add to the growth of the hobby.

The most popular language of the microcomputer is undoubtedly the high level version known as BASIC and for most devotees of the hobby it has become accepted as the norm if not the only way to 'talk' to their machine. This is understandable in view of the comparative friendliness of the language together with the ease with which the neophyte can produce useful results within an hour or so of the initial purchase. The more 'noble' languages such as PASCAL and ALGOL tend to be neglected due to a combination of reasons including financial. Few home computers have the necessary translating software to handle these languages so extra expenditure is required as well as the intellectual effort involved in mastering fresh syntax laws.

There is, however, in all computers an obscure alternative language — machine code. It is provided free, executes at lightning speed and is ultra efficient in terms of memory usage. Machine code enables you to converse *directly* with the most important silicon chip in your machine which is of course the *microprocessor*.

This book may stimulate your interest in the subject and help in overcoming the initial inertia. It deals exclusively with the particular microprocessor having the type number 6502 (and 6502A) and is found in many popular microcomputers including the APPLE, PET, ACORN, ATARI and last but not least, the BBC system. Machine code is not easy to learn so the examples which accompany the text deliberately err on the side of simplicity. I have discovered to my cost that machine code is certainly not easy to write about without introducing at least some of the awesome jargon which surrounds the subject. If you survive this book you would be well advised to study the numerous advanced works available on 6502 code.

My thanks are due to my dear wife Mabs who suffered many hours of a clicking typewriter without complaint and also to the Editor of *Computing Today* who gave me the initial confidence to write at all on the subject.

A.P.S.

Contents

1

The native language of the computer

Why learn machine code?

The dramatic fall in cost, the pressures of the advertising media and the profusion of technical magazines now available has caused more and more people to buy a microcomputer either for themselves or for their children. Computer enthusiasts are being created at an ever increasing rate and are threatening to outnumber even bingo and football enthusiasts.

When you join the ranks of the computing fraternity you will first have to learn how to deal with outsiders who delight in posing what they consider to be a highly original question 'what can you actually *do* with one of these things?' Probably you will decide to join one of the many computer clubs which are springing up in most towns and where the most varied assortment of humanity collects on one or more evenings a week. Some will subject you to the exciting details of a new add-on gadget, others will make your brain reel with the latest computing buzzwords. Almost certainly you will hear arguments (usually quite fierce) on the respective merits and demerits of PASCAL, BASIC, COMAL and FORTH etc. There will however be one or two present who appear to attract a certain amount of respect. On enquiry, you will be told, in rather a hushed voice, that they know machine code. You gather from this that an ability to 'know' machine code almost qualifies you for entrance to the Royal Enclosure at Ascot. The question which arises is whether or not such adulation is justified?

The vast majority of home computer owners start on BASIC because, rightly or wrongly, this is the resident language in ROM and once proficiency is gained it is not easy to budge from it. It is true that some writers derive a certain amount of satisfaction from deriding BASIC. According to Dijkstra, an eminent intellectual in the world of computing science (and incidentally a bit of a snob), '. . . any student that had a prior exposure to BASIC would be mentally mutilated beyond hope of regeneration'. Few, of course, except his admiring followers, would take such a remark seriously though they may applaud his attempt to emulate the wit of Oscar Wilde. It would be unprofitable in a book on machine code to enter into the respective virtues of the various high level languages. The strength of these arguments is diluted by emotion and prejudice in many cases although they do provide interesting reading as an alternative to watching the nth repeat of *Casablanca*. What is important is to discuss the advantages or otherwise of machine code versus *all other high level languages*.

We start with the bad news. Machine code is difficult, frustrating and shows up the computer for what it is — a silicon moron! Users of high level language may be excused for falling into the trap of thinking that computers are 'smart' although there is certainly no excuse for thinking they are 'intelligent'. Any property of the computer that appears to deserve the label 'intelligence' must be attributed to the sophistication of the resident software which is *man's* doing — using 'man' in the generic sense which includes woman. This mass of software, interposed between you and the crudities of machine code, allows you to control powerful operations by simply typing in the appropriate keyword. For example, the simple BASIC line PRINT A, which we all take for granted as performing the simple task of placing a number on the screen at the current cursor position, when analysed into its machine code equivalent would probably surprise or maybe even frighten you. The newcomer to machine code soon realises that the microprocessor, the 'miracle chip' beloved by the media, is a miracle only because it has thousands of circuits buried within a small slab of silicon. All it can do is to add or subtract two numbers at a time (provided they are very small), count up and down and move bits around from one part of the system to another although, to be fair, at a truly phenomenal speed.

After this depressing introduction to machine code it must come as a relief to learn that the other side of the coin is more cheerful. The advantages are listed here (but not necessarily in order of importance) using BASIC as the yardstick for comparison:

1. *Speed of execution*
   A program written in machine code will probably execute many times faster, perhaps as much as a hundred or more times faster. This is because you are conversing in the computer's *native* language instead of circumventing the translation software. Another reason for the enhanced speed is the *dedication* of the coding to the particular objective rather than employing translation subroutines which must be *general purpose* orientated and therefore wasteful in code. As an example, if the program only intends to use the top line of the screen area for textual purposes the coding is tailor made for just this requirement; a general purpose translation segment would probably cater for text to be displayed at any desired part of the

screen and must therefore contain redundant code in many cases of use.

2. *Memory economy*

A machine code program, if sensibly written, is economical in the use of memory for the same basic reasons given under speed above. A floating point number in BASIC is often stored in *five* bytes of memory irrespective of its magnitude! Thus if you want to store the number 3 it will occupy as much memory 'real estate' as storing the number 33333333 or even 3.567843×10^{23}. With machine code, memory allocation can be tightly allocated according to the magnitude of a number. Another memory saving is achieved because there is no need to store BASIC line numbers or keep track of keyword lists. Keywords like LET or PRINT are easy for humans but quite incomprehensible to the machine code vocabulary so their translation wastes memory space.

3. *Input/output control*

Most children from the age of six to sixty like seeing things move. One of the fascinating properties of a computing system is the ability to control not only the conventional peripherals such as printers, tape recorders, floppy disks etc., but also mechanical models and various home or commercially made gadgets. This exercise demands some knowledge of the input/output ports and in many cases BASIC is not ideally suited for such purposes due mainly to the slow response to input and output line signals.

4. *Screen dynamics*

Programs which produce moving 'pictures' such as in 'space war' type games are greatly improved in machine code versions.

5. *Ego boosting*

This is a trivial, superficial advantage but many of us, including the writer, are basically egotists and secretly enjoy inflicting awe on people. In any case, you may like your name to be mentioned 'in a hushed voice' at the local computer club.

The overriding advantage of learning machine code however is the satisfaction of knowing a little more about the true workings of a computer instead of through the rose tinted spectacles of a high level language which demands virtually no knowledge whatsoever of the machine architecture. It may be argued that it is not necessary to know how say, a watch works in order to use it, but if computing is a hobby the argument is unconvincing because all aspects of the subject should be equally interesting. Although the computer employs electronics, it is possible to gain quite a detailed knowledge of the inner workings of a computer without any prior knowledge of electronics. This is because the digital computer is simply a *two-state* system and only two electrical levels are encountered, voltage or no-voltage. The general principle would be the same if a computer ran on gas instead of electricity, the two states would then be gas or no-gas. The rest of this chapter covers some of the preliminary work necessary to embark on machine code programming. If you already own a home computer, most of this information may already be available to you in the User Manual, but it will probably be a little too specific to the particular machine and therefore lacking in generality.

The microcomputer system

The major components in a microcomputer system consist of the microprocessor chip, a few memory chips, one or more chips to communicate with the external peripherals, a power supply and an oscillator called the 'clock'. The remaining components are a heterogeneous assortment of chips which come under the heading of logic support. The number of these support chips is beginning to thin out in some of the modern machines due to a technique known as *uncommitted logic arrays* or more simply, ULAs. This allows much of the support logic to be cheaply integrated into one or two ULA chips, lowering the total chip count and therefore improving the overall reliability of the system. The famous ZX81 has a very low chip count owing to the use of ULAs and the powerful BBC/ACORN machine has also incorporated the technique. Fig. 1.1 shows the simplified overview of the microcomputer system in sufficient detail to cover present purposes.

The components of the system in Fig. 1.1 have the following duties:

1. *The microprocessor chip*
   This is the central processor of the computing system and has complete control of all other components. The primary function is to *interpret* machine code instructions and *execute* them in the required order. It must be emphasised that the machine code is *specific* to the particular microprocessor type — it cannot 'understand' other microprocessor codes.

2. *Memory chips*
   The microprocessor can only execute a program if the machine code instructions (which form that program) are already stored somewhere in memory. There are two kinds of memory chips:

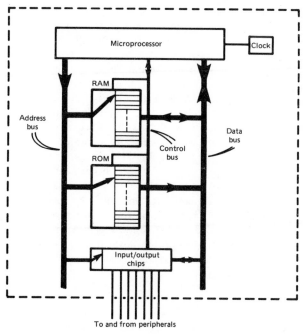

Fig. 1.1. Simplified microcomputer system

(a) RAM (Random Access Memory)
    Information can be stored or changed in RAM. Storing new
    information in a RAM is called *writing*; finding out what is
    already in RAM is called *reading*.

    Remember this: | writing new information destroys the old
                   | information; reading information does not
                   | destroy existing information.

(b) ROM (Read Only Memory)
    Information in ROM is permanent and placed there during
    manufacture. It is impossible for the microprocessor to change
    the contents of a ROM, i.e., you cannot write into a ROM.

The term RAM is an unwise choice of terminology because strictly
both RAMs and ROMs are 'random access' in the sense that any
particular piece of information can be accessed, irrespective of *where*
it is in the chip. The preferable term would have been RWM (Read
Write Memory) but the modern craze for twisting abbreviations to
form acronyms appears to be more important than the conveyed
sense.

One other primary distinguishing factor between RAMs and ROMs is the property of *volatility*. A memory is said to be volatile if the security of the stored information depends on the application of power. The information in a RAM is volatile — it 'evaporates' if the power is interrupted even for a split second. ROMs do not rely on a sustained power supply so are described as *non-volatile*. Bearing this in mind should resolve the problem, 'what kind of stuff goes in RAM and what kind goes in ROM?'. In practice, the typical home computer will have one or more ROMs which have been pre-programmed with the operating system software, a complex set of programs which enables the user to sit at the keyboard and control the computer. The programs will include a high level language translator (almost always BASIC) and probably a *machine code monitor* for entering your programs in machine code. As far as the RAM is concerned almost the whole of it is yours! Any programs you enter whether in machine code or BASIC will go into the RAM space. If you have an important program in RAM it is of course up to you to save it on tape (or disk) *before* switching off the machine — remember that RAM is volatile!

3. *The address bus and the data bus*

Fig. 1.1 shows two thick bundles of wire which appear to connect the RAMs and ROMs to the microprocessor. The term *bus* implies a set of wires have a commonly related purpose so we distinguish an *address* bus and a *data* bus.

(a) The address bus

This is used by the microprocessor to select one particular *location* in the memory system. Memory chips may be considered as a collection of separate locations (pigeon holes). Each location is uniquely defined by an *address code*. The pattern of binary zeros and ones on the address bus causes an electronic 'arm' to move to the particular location, thus identifying it for action by the system. The arm shown in the RAM and ROM of Fig. 1.1 is of course an oversimplification, it will in fact be a chunk of electronic circuitry located within the memory chip and called a *decoder*. As far as the address bus is concerned it has no way of knowing whether the address code refers to RAM or ROM. Only one location can be selected at any one time by the system so locations, whether in RAM or ROM, must not have overlapping address codes. The number of wires on the address bus is normally sixteen. The number of different binary patterns possible on the address bus is 2^{16} or 65 536. This is because the law of combinations is defined by the formula

number of combinations = 2^N where N is the number of wires.

To save referring to the awkward decimal numbers which crop up in binary, the number 65 536 is more easily remembered as 64K, one 'K' in binary being 2^{10} which is 1024. It follows from the previous comments that however much money you can spend on memory chips, you cannot hang more than a total of 64K on the address bus. (Some of the latest microprocessors have increased the number of address wires to 22 which allows a total addressing space of 2^{22} or over 4 million addresses!)

(b) The data bus

When we have mentioned 'information' stored in a location there has been no explanation given as to the *amount* of information which each location can hold — how many binary bits? In most current microprocessors, the standard is eight bits which is known as the *word length*. Thus the 'width' of each memory location is eight bits, commonly called a *byte*. The object of the data bus is to provide a highway between the selected memory location and the microprocessor and must therefore be a bunch of eight wires with each wire dedicated to the passage of one bit. The bytes are thus transmitted to or from memory via the medium of the data bus. You will notice from Fig. 1.1 that the data bus is bidirectional because of the requirements of RAM. As far as the ROM is concerned, the data bus only appears as a one-way path, *from* ROM *to* microprocessor.

4. *The control bus*

Unlike the previous two bus systems, the control bus is a hotchpotch of single wires, each having a completely unrelated function to the others. Thus it is incorrectly called a 'bus'. No information (in the normal meaning of the term) is carried by the control wires, they serve only as trigger lines to activate the various components at the right time. One of these will be the R/W or *read/write* line which informs the RAM when to read and when to write. The remaining control wires will not be discussed at this stage.

5. *The clock*

The microprocessor requires a set of timing pulses to synchronise all the components in the system. These pulses are generated by the so-called *clock* chip. (In some microprocessors, the clock circuitry is integrated within the microprocessor chip.)

6. *The input/output chips*

These are used to provide an *interface* between the computing components and the external components or *peripherals*. The term

7

interface is used to describe any device which must be interposed between two systems in order to compensate for their incompatibility. Peripherals are items such as keyboards, monitor screens, printers, cassette tape units, light pens etc. The incompatibility may be due to different electrical requirements (different voltage or current levels) or simply a timing problem. Peripherals, as far as the computer is concerned, are undisciplined and lethargic. Computers operate on a microsecond time scale, whereas peripherals muddle along at a sluggish millisecond pace — some of them, human operated keyboards for example, have difficulty in cracking the 0.1 second barrier! Because of the timing discrepancies, peripherals are, in general, not synchronised to the computer clock; they are said to operate *asynchronously*.

Input/output chips can be quite complex, having built in sophistication to deal, as far as possible, with a wide range of peripheral equipment. They may have exotic names like 'Peripheral Interface Adaptor' or 'Versatile Interface Adaptor' but they all feature a bunch of input/output wires for passing data and some control wires called 'handshake lines'. There are two rival protocols for peripheral organisation:

(a) Special instructions
    The machine code repertoire includes instructions which act specifically on the input/output chips.

(b) Memory mapping
    No special instructions exist to handle input/output chips. The microprocessor considers the input/output data lines as *ordinary memory locations*. Memory mapping tends to be the more favoured system because of the inherent flexibility. Each input/output chip has its own unique set of addresses on the 64K memory 'map' and there can be a large number of such chips in a system. Fig. 1.1 assumes a memory mapped system because of the address 'arm' shown.

Manipulations with binary

Numbers expressed in binary appear cumbersome and uninformative after an upbringing geared to the decimal notation. Because of this, BASIC and most other high level languages provide you with 99% protection against the ravages of binary by pretending it doesn't exist. They provide convenient translation routines so that you can continue thinking in decimal. Nevertheless, the computer is by nature a digital beast and can digest binary with relish. Unfortunately, machine code programming does demand some dexterity in the manipulation of binary patterns together with a moderate fluency in binary arithmetic. Those readers who are already proficient in binary can skip the remainder of this chapter. The less endowed types must grit their teeth (like I had to) and stick with it.

Binary patterns

A *bit* is a binary '1' or a '0'. A binary *string* is a collection of bits. A string of eight bits is now known as a *byte*. A byte is conveniently treated in two halves; each four-bit half is called a *nibble*.

The following notation is popular for referring to particular bits within a byte

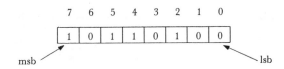

The example byte is shown as a partitioned box. The bit positions are labelled *bit 0* (the rightmost position) to bit 7. The terms 'least significant bit' or lsb and the 'most significant bit' or msb are special labels for bits at each end. The left hand nibble in the example is 1011 and the right hand nibble is 0100.

It is often necessary to consider two bytes 'joined together' in which case they are distinguished by calling one of them the *higher order* byte and the other the *lower order* byte.

RAM and ROM store their information in bytes, one addressable location holds one byte. If the particular item of information cannot be accommodated within the confines of one byte it must occupy two or more *contiguous* locations. The dictionary defines contiguous as 'following in order' from which we deduce that in this sense it means occupying adjacently addressed locations.

It is time we dug a little deeper into the computer meaning of the harmless word 'information'. What information is contained in a byte of bits? The strange answer is — anything the programmer wishes it to mean! We should realise that automatically assuming that a string of bits must be considered a binary *number* is misguided. It could, for example, be simply a code. It could be an abbreviated form of quite detailed information concerning an employee. If it does represent a number there are several different ways of expressing the same number as the following will show.

(a) Unsigned binary

The bit positions represent the power of 2 in ascending order from

9

lsb to msb. A '1' means that power of 2 is present, a '0' means it is absent. Thus, 00010101 would represent the number 21 in decimal

$$\begin{array}{r} 1 \\ 4 \\ 16 \\ \hline 21 \end{array}$$

The bit positions in a byte are 1 2 4 8 16 32 64 128 (from right to left). Examples are better than explanations:

10000001 = 129   00000111 = 7   10101010 = 170   11111111 = 255

The last example is a special case since it is often required to quickly estimate the highest number which can be held in a string of N bits. Instead of collecting the individual bit powers, the following rule can be used.

> Largest unsigned number which can be held in a string of N bits is $2^N - 1$

Thus 11111111 is $2^8 - 1$ = 255 decimal.

So we must conclude that the largest number which can be held in one memory location is 255 decimal. If however the programmer decides to allocate two adjacent locations to hold one number (by considering them to be joined end to end) the largest number now would be 11111111 11111111 which by the previous rule would give us the number $2^{16} - 1$ = 65 536 − 1 = 65 535.

(b) Signed binary and two's complement

If both positive and negative numbers are to be represented then one bit must be wasted to indicate the sign. This is always the msb and the remaining seven bits must represent the magnitude. Positive numbers have sign 0, negative 1.

Example:
01100011 is a positive number; 10010010 is a negative number.

sign bit   sign bit

For positive numbers, the form is straightforward, thus 00000111 = + 7. Negative numbers however are far from straightforward because they are represented by a method know as *two's complement*.

10

The two's complement of a number is found by first reversing all the bits and then adding 1.

Example: 00000111 is + 7.   Now reverse the bits,
          11111000   now add 1,
          11111001 is then −7.

Example: 00000100 is + 4.   Reversing the bits,
          11111011   now add 1,
          11111100 is then −4.

To avoid the error prone exercise of adding 1 (it is easy to forget a carry) an alternative way to obtain the two's complement is:

> Start from the right. Copy down without change up to and inclusive of the first '1' and thereafter change the bits.

Example: positive number   00001101
         two's complement 11110011

Note the method is also valid the other way round; the two's complement of a negative number is the equivalent positive number.

Since there are only seven bits to represent the magnitude, the largest positive number which can be held in a byte is +127 (2^7-1). The largest negative number is one more, −128, which seems surprising.

Another quirk is the upside down appearance of negative numbers because the smallest negative number looks like the largest. Consider the number (−1). Since 00000001 is +1 then from the previous rule 11111111 is −1. Note that if the byte was intended to be treated as an unsigned binary number, it would represent 255 instead of −1. The following analysis of a 3-bit word may help in understanding the curious behaviour of two's complement numbers.

0	0	0	0
0	0	1	+ 1
0	1	0	+ 2
0	1	1	+ 3
1	0	0	−4
1	0	1	−3
1	1	0	−2
1	1	1	−1

Since '0' is a *positive* number it means there are four positive numbers and four negative numbers. This explains why there appears to be 'one more' negative number.

11

There is a final question to be answered before leaving the subject of two's complement. Why is such an ungainly system used? It is simply a case of the economics of computer circuitry. Two's complement allows the arithmetic circuits of a computer to be limited to performing *addition*. Subtraction can then be treated as a special case of addition by the trick of adding a negative number — which is the same as subtraction. Finally, why two's complement? Whats wrong with 'one's complement'?

The one's complement of a number (sometimes called the *logical complement*) is simply the number with all the bits reversed or *complemented*.

Thus, 01010101 has a one's complement (logical complement) of 10101010.

The two's complement is of course obtained by *adding one more*. Why the one's complement is seldom used is because of certain ambiguities which arise, such as two different ways of representing zero — which would be disastrous.

Thus 00000000 would represent zero (plus zero)

then 11111111 would represent minus zero. This could be fatal in a computing system. However by using the two's complement, the extra one kicks all those 1s back to 0s.

Thus 11111111 is the one's complement of zero but by adding 1,

$$1$$

$1 \leftarrow \boxed{00000000}$ it can be seen that the propagation of the carry leaves the eight zeros which is respectable and normal. The carry that is kicked out of the system at the msb end is ignored; it can't be held in a byte anyway!

(c) Binary coded decimal (BCD)

This representation of a number is a kind of compromise between the conflicting interests of humans and computers. It is easier to associate the binary string with the world of real decimal numbers if BCD is used. BCD allows a byte to be considered as two separate nibbles, each nibble representing an independent decimal digit according to simple binary powers.

To understand BCD consider the byte 00100111,
split into two nibbles 0010 0111,
now read this as   27   decimal.

Because of the four-bit binary form it is easy to translate into the equivalent decimal almost at sight. Note that in the above example its decimal value in unsigned binary is a tougher proposition — 39 decimal. There is one further point to be made on BCD with regard to illegal combinations — there are six of them in each nibble. The largest decimal digit is 9 which means that the binary combinations

1010, 1011, 1100, 1101, 1110 and 1111 are forbidden combinations. Because of the six illegals which exist in BCD, it may be seen that the form is inherently wasteful of memory storage capacity because although these illegals are unused, they inhabit phantom positions within the byte. To illustrate the wastage we recall that the largest number held in unsigned binary in one byte is equivalent to 255 decimal whereas in BCD, the largest decimal is 99. Thus we have to allocate more storage capacity if BCD is used. The main area of BCD usage is when dealing with computer controlled instrumentation. Such instruments have INPUT/OUTPUT lines which feed or receive data in BCD format.

Some microprocessors can perform arithmetic on either two's complement numbers or can be programmed to accept BCD numbers direct and produce the result in BCD. Fortunately, the 6502 is equipped for this operation.

Hexadecimal code

This subject is treated separately from the previous binary manipulations because it is simply a code used to identify or *describe* a binary string of bits. Describing a binary string by its decimal equivalent is not rapid enough — even with practice could you almost *instantly* say what is 11011011 in decimal? BCD is easier but we are then faced with the six illegals for which we have no symbol.

Hexadecimal or simply 'hex' uses the full sixteen characters to describe the binary contents of a nibble (the base of hexadecimal is sixteen).

The characters in hex are 0, 1, 2, 3, 4, 5, 6, 7, 8, 9, A, B, C, D, E, F.

The letters start where the numbers finish so A is ten, B is eleven and so on until we reach F which is fifteen. One hex digit describes one nibble so to describe a byte we need *two hex digits*. Here are some examples:

01110001	11111111	10101010	10110000	00000000	00001111
71	FF	AA	BO	00	OF

Hex is very important in machine code programming and it must be learned. The microprocessor set of instruction codes are given in hex. Addresses are given in hex as well as decimal; strangely, an address in hex tends to be easier to comprehend than the equivalent decimal when relating it to the system address bus. If we label the addresses in decimal the range is from 0 to 65 535. If we use hex, we only need four hex characters to cover the range. The lowest address is 0000 and the highest address is FFFF because if the sixteen address lines are all at

'1', the highest address must be 1111 1111 1111 1111 which is FFFF in hex.

Although hex is used primarily for descriptive rather than arithmetic purposes, it is often necessary to count in hex. The base of decimal is 10, the base of binary is 2 but the base of hex is 16. This means that every hex digit ascends in powers of 16 from right to left and we visualise that each digit sits underneath its respective power as follows:

	16^3	16^2	16	1	
					, but it is better to think
in this form	4096	256	16	1	. As an example, the
hex number	1	2	5	F	can be evaluated as follows:
15×1				15	
5×16				80	
2×256				512	
1×4096				4096	
				4703	decimal

Associated with hex is the concept of dividing the 64K memory map into *pages*.

> One page is 256 bytes of memory

Bearing this in mind, it is convenient to visualise a four-hex digit numbered address as follows:

Page number ⎯⎯⎯⎯⎯⎤ ⎡⎯⎯⎯⎯⎯ address within page

$$\underset{\sim}{X} \underset{\sim}{X} \underset{\sim}{X} \underset{\sim}{X}$$

Example: the address 0305 refers to address 05 on page 03.
Example: the address FFFF refers to address FF on page FF.

Most microprocessors attach special significance to page zero which is the range 0000 to 00FF. In the 6502 some instructions are lumped under the heading of 'page zero' instructions and will only operate within the boundaries of this page. Page one in the 6502 is also 'special' since it is the area dedicated to a powerful memory block known as the *stack*. Page one extends between the limits 0100 to 01FF.

Adding in hex is weird until you get used to it. It is best to quote some examples rather than a formal description:

F
4
―――
13   Check: $15 + 4 = 19$ decimal which is $3 + (1 \times 16) = 13$ hex

You have to remember that in any column, if a total exceeds F there must be a carry to the next higher order column.

Here are some more examples of adding two hex numbers:

F	FF	CE	FFF
A	01	15	101
19	100	E3	1100

It was mentioned earlier that the highest positive number in a two's complement byte is $+127$ which is the string 01111111. Quoting this in hex, it is 7F. Thus it is useful to remember that:

Highest positive number is 7F

Any hex number 'larger' than 7F tips the number over to the negative region. Thus the hex number FF, which you may be excused for thinking is a 'large' number, is indeed only numerically equal to -1. This point is worth mentioning because forgetting this may lead to an erroneous check when you later substitute sample data in order to prove that your addition program is valid.

This about concludes the background information necessary to embark on the perilous but satisfying road to machine code programming.

Summary

- Machine code is difficult but is worth learning.
- Programs written in machine code execute faster, take less memory space, improve screen dynamics and could increase your standing(?).
- It enables you to understand the internal operation of computers whereas high-level languages such as BASIC are undemanding in this respect.
- The computer operates as a two-state system: the two states can be called 1 and 0 or high and low or volts and no-volts or indeed any other pair of opposites . . . even New York and Moscow if the mood takes you.
- A microprocessor by itself is not a computing system. It requires memory chips, input/output chips, a clock and various peripherals.
- The microprocessor controls the system, the ROMs and RAMs store the information, the address bus decides which piece of information, the data bus carries the information back and forth.

- The address bus in the 6502 has 16 wires so is thus capable of 2^{16} different address codes.
- The data bus is always as 'wide' as memory. In the 6502 it is 8 bits.
- Eight bits is called a byte which in turn consists of two 4-bit nibbles.
- Input/output chips are designed to ease the problems associated with peripheral interfacing.
- The 6502 employs a memory-mapped input/output system so there are no special instructions to activate peripherals . . . they are treated no differently to an addressed memory location.
- The term 'bit' means either a '1' or a '0'. The bits within a byte are referred to as bit 0 through to 7. The least significant bit is 'bit 0'.
- Two bytes considered joined are distinguished by 'lower order and higher order' bytes.
- A string of bits can mean many different things, depending on the programmer's viewpoint.
- An unsigned binary number uses all the bits for representing magnitude. The highest number held in a byte is 255 decimal.
- Signed binary numbers normally employ the two's complement notation where the msb is reserved for the sign bit. 0 = positive; 1 = negative.
- The largest positive two's complement number within a byte is +127: the largest negative is −128.
- BCD is useful for instrumentation input/output devices.
- There are six illegal combinations in a BCN nibble, 1010 to 1111.
- Hex coding is basically a descriptive code used widely in machine code literature. The characters are the numbers 0 through to 9 and the letters A through to F. The base of the hex code is sixteen.
- A four hex-digit address can cover the entire range of a 16-bit addressing scheme.
- A 'page' of memory is 256 bytes. Page 0 is 0000 to 00FF.
- The two right hand hex digits is the address within a page. The left hand two hex digits is the page number.
- There are 256 pages in the total 64K memory map.
- RAMs can have their contents changed by programmed instructions but the information stored is volatile.
- ROMs have fixed information and are non-volatile.

2

Architecture of the 6502

Family history

The first microprocessor was inflicted on an innocent society in the year 1971 by Intel. After a short time, two rival species dominated the market. These were the Intel 8080 and the Motorola 6800, both of which began to sell in enormous quantities and were second sourced under licence by many other manufacturers. Keeping the overall pattern of the 8080 reasonably intact, Zilog added many more instructions and produced an upgraded model which has retained popularity to the present day — the famous Z80. The Z80 was designed to retain compatibility with the 8080 by including the original instruction set plus extras. In this way, it was possible for programs originally written for the 8080 to be still run on the Z80. It is worth mentioning at this point that the currently popular disk operating system known as CP/M, although commonly supposed to operate only with a Z80 based machine, assumes only the original 8080 instructions to be present. Our 6502 microprocessor has the Motorola 6800 microprocessor as its ancestor and was desgined by MOS Technology The 6502 is used in many popular microcomputers including the Apple, Pet, Acorn Atom, Atari, Aim 65 and last, but certainly not least, the BBC microcomputer.

The 6502 has many powerful features but sadly, one or two annoying ones.

Internal anatomy

A detailed drawing of the various bits and pieces within the chip would be not only confusing but quite unnecessary from the point of view of the machine code programmer. It is sufficient to understand the functions of those registers which are programmable. The term *register* is used for a set of electronic 'switches' which can store a set of binary bits until such time as they are needed. Registers are therefore similar to memory locations which we have previously discussed except they

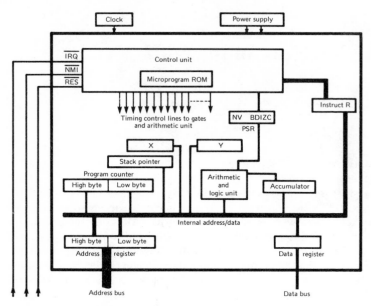

Fig. 2.1. Simplified interior view of the 6502 microprocessor chip

are *inside* the microprocessor itself. They are constructed differently from memory cells in order to increase the storage and retrieval time and they may have more sophisticated control circuitry. Their functions extend beyond that of mere storage since they must take their part in the role of program execution. Fig. 2.1 shows a simplified version of the registers within the 6502 and the interconnections between each.

The accumulator (A)

This, from the programmer's viewpoint, is the most important register in the chip since it is the only one equipped to carry out complex operations. If you wish to add two numbers together for instance, they must be read from memory in turn and passed to the accumulator. You cannot add directly to memory locations. Some ideas of its status can be gained by noting the special connection between it and the block called the Arithmetic and Logic Unit (ALU). It is not proposed to deal with the intricacies of the ALU because the programmer will be unaware of its existence. In all fairness to the ALU however, it should be pointed out that this is the place where all the real work of processing is carried out — the accumulator only *appears* important to the programmer. The accumulator, like most of the other registers in the chip, is one byte wide.

Summarising the role of the accumulator we can liken it to a Motion at a Conference. At a conference, 'all Motions must be passed through the Chair' but within a microcomputer, all data must be passed through the accumulator!

The X and Y registers (X, Y)

These registers have two distinct functions. Either of them can serve as temporary holding registers for dumping information. There are times when the accumulator may have valuable information but it is required for other purposes. Instructions exist for transferring the contents of the accumulator to the X or Y registers or transferring back again.

A more important function is concerned with a technique known as indexed addressing, the details of which will be mercifully left to a later chapter. Facilities exist also for using the registers as counters. No addition or subtraction can be performed.

The stack-pointer (S)

The *stack* is described in detail later. It is sufficient at this time to define it as a general purpose dumping ground. It is not in the microprocessor. It is an area in the external RAM memory occupying a maximum of 256 bytes (or one 'page') and *always situated in page one*. The exact position at which the stack starts is decided by the programmer in the first instance by *loading* (writing) a number into the stack pointer. This number is interpreted as the address of the stack. Once this chore has been accomplished, the behaviour of the stack is subsequently automatic because the stack pointer is *decremented* (contents reduced by 1) after each dumping operation, so the next dump can take place in a fresh location. When retrieving data from the stack, the reverse process is activated; the stack pointer is first *incremented* so as to point back to the address of the last data item entered. The stack is called a Last In First Out or LIFO memory because the last data entered must be the first to be recalled.

The stack pointer is for all practical purposes one byte wide so it can seemingly only serve as an address pointer over the range 00 to FF hex (page zero). But as previously stated, the stack can only be on page *one*. This ambiguity is resolved by the neat dodge of wiring in a ninth bit stuck permanently at '1' at the msb end of the stack pointer; the effective address range then being 100 to 1FF which are the page one boundaries.

The Processor Status Register (P)

This is not a register under the normal meaning of the term. It is not a general purpose storage cell for data. It is a set of individual *flag* bits used to record (remember) certain incidents which have taken place in the immediate past. A flag bit is one which is effectively a yes/no signal. The particular incident which is flagged depends on the position within the PSR. The register is the customary eight bits wide but one of the bit positions is unused:

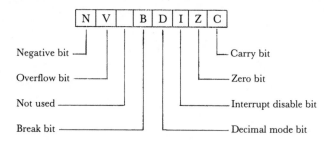

The N, V, B, Z and C flags are automatically set to '1' or reset to '0' depending on the result of a recently executed instruction; in most cases, the immediate recent. The rule in translation is that a '1' means yes or 'true' whereas a '0' means no or 'false'. For example, if the N bit is 1 the previous instruction must have resulted in a negative number (the msb must have been 1).

You may be wondering to whom is this fascinating information directed? Why are the flags important? The information is required by the microprocessor *decision* circuits when dealing with the machine code equivalent to the IF THEN statements of BASIC. Later, the details of branch type instructions will be given such as BMI which means 'branch if minus'. This means in effect 'branch to some out of sequence for the next instruction *if* the *last result* was negative' — in other words, if the N bit was set. The V bit is set as a result of an add or subtract process leading to an overflow condition, while the C bit is set if a carry resulted. The C bit may under certain circumstances be considered as a ninth bit tacked on to the end of a register or memory location. It should be pointed out provisionally that a carry out from a register does not necessarily indicate an overflow condition — one of the quirks of two's complement arithmetic discussed in more detail later. In case this may appear worrying consider the case of adding 1 to −1:

$$
\begin{array}{ll}
11111111 & (-1)
\end{array}
$$

$$
\boxed{\text{C}} \qquad\qquad\qquad 1 \qquad (+1)
$$

$$
1 \longleftarrow \boxed{00000000}
$$

Note that a carry was generated into the C bit but the result is a valid one, so there is no overflow status to be signalled.

Most of the PSR bits are programmable, i.e. they can be set or reset by special instructions.

The D bit may be set to 1 by the programmer if the numbers entering the arithmetic unit are intended to be treated in BCD format (refer back to Chapter 1). Once the D bit is set to 1, all subsequent arithmetic proceeds on the assumption of BCD inputs until such time as the programmer resets the D bit back again to 0. It is up to the programmer to ensure that illegal BCD groups are not presented.

The I bit is also programmable and is set to 1 (by an instruction) if for some reason or other, an 'interrupt request' is to be denied. An *interrupt* is a method of literally interrupting the current program execution in order to deal with a peripheral device. For certain parts of a current program, it would be embarrassing for an interrupt to be allowed so the programmer can arrange for critical areas to be immune to peripheral attack. The B bit is set to 1 if the program is interrupted by a 'break' command (BRK).

Interrupt Signals

These are RESet, Interrupt ReQuest and Non Maskable Interrupt. There are three control wires on the microprocessor (see Fig. 2.1) marked RES, IRQ, NMI from which interrupts can occur. Notice the convention of the *negator bar* over the top of a pin label which indicates that inverted logic (sometimes called active LOW signal) is required. Thus a ground or LOW level voltage initiates the action instead of a HIGH voltage (this information is only interesting to electronic hardware enthusiasts).

RES action: When this pin is grounded, all activity in the system stops — the microprocessor goes on strike! When this ground is released and the pin is brought HIGH again, the following actions occur:

1. The address bus is forced by the Program Counter (treated

21

later) to adopt the hex number FFFC and then FFFD. The contents of these two locations are then interpreted as the address from where the first instruction is to be taken.

2. The I bit in the PSR is set to prevent interrupts.
3. The processing of all instructions in memory (from the first onwards) commences.

It is of course necessary for the programmer to ensure that the addresses FFFC and FFFD contain the two byte address of the 'first instruction'. In a typical computer system, this area of the memory will be pre-programmed in a ROM forming part of the resident *operating system*. Reset action is intended to ensure the system powers up in an orderly fashion. Since the term 'system' includes the peripherals, the input/output chips also have a RES pin which is connected to the microprocessor's pin. The registers within the typical input/output chips are normally set to all zeros under reset conditions. On the other hand, the registers within the microprocessor are not zeroed. With the exception of the I bit (which is set to 1) the contents of all registers is mere garbage under reset conditions and it is the responsibility of the operating system software designer to organise the initial contents by suitable instructions in the ROM.

IRQ action: When a peripheral requests service it sets a flag bit situated inside the input/output chip. If the I bit in the microprocessor PSR is reset (0), it is allowed to interrupt. The procedure is:

1. The address bus is forced to FFFE and then FFFF. The contents of these two locations are interpreted as the address of the first instruction of *another* program designed to service the peripheral. After the interrupted program has its *current position* stored in the stack, the other program begins to execute. This other program is called an *interrupt routine*.
2. When the interrupt routine is finished, the processor retrieves the return address from the stack again and the main program continues from the point at which it was interrupted.

As previously stated, the interrupt request will not take place if the I bit is set. However, if the I bit is subsequently reset and the flag in the input/output chip is still set, the interrupt is belatedly serviced.

NMI action. Unlike IRQ, NMI is not subservient to the I bit — it is a brute force action with no breeding or manners. It just barges into whatever else is going on, jumping to its own special program and, as explained before, returning control to the main program when completed.

The address lines are forced to FFFA and FFFB on receipt of the interrupt.

Understandably, the manufacturers of home computers either warn you against tampering with $\overline{\text{NMI}}$ or prevent your access to the pin.

Jump vectors

Machine code programmers in the home computer environment will want to experiment with $\overline{\text{IRQ}}$, particularly if the objective is the control of electromechanical models. There is one mystery to resolve concerning the earlier references to the special memory addresses dedicated to the servicing of interrupts.

For example, the $\overline{\text{IRQ}}$ address in ROM must be at address FFFE and FFFF. But if it is in ROM the home programmer can't get to it! How can we use $\overline{\text{IRQ}}$ to jump to our own interrupt service routine if it is permanently hogged by the resident operating system?

In most systems, the user is allowed access by reason of a simple piece of trickery which we shall call a *jump vector*. The operating system usually ensures that the contents of FFFE and FFFF contain an address in RAM. At this address is an instruction which is a JUMP instruction to the start of the operating system program. Thus the system arrives by an intermediate stepping stone in RAM. The address of the jump vector in RAM will be (or ought to be) given in the User's Manual. To use interrupt, all you have to do is to store the contents, replace the contents by your own jump vector (which will now point to the start of your program) and finally replace the original contents which belonged to the operating system.

The Program Counter (PC)

This is the prima donna of all the registers but, apart from one instruction 'NO OPERATION', it is not directly programmable. The course of all programs is completely under the control of the program counter so its function is worth special treatment:

> The program counter contains the address of the *next* instruction byte to be fetched from memory.

After each instruction byte is fetched from memory, the program counter is *incremented,* from which we assume that instructions are executed in strict address order.

There is one exception to the contiguous-address rhythm. If the currently accessed instruction is a conditional BRANCH IF type and the condition is indeed true, an entirely *new number* is placed into the program counter. Thus the next instruction byte is fetched from an entirely different address decided by the programmer. The normal action of the program counter continues again from this fresh address.

The program counter must be able to reach any part of the 64K memory space and consequently must be capable of holding a four hex digit address. The register may be considered in two parts, the *higher order* byte (PCH) and the *lower order* byte (PCL).

Example:

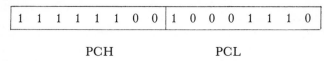

PCH is holding FC and PCL is holding 8E; the combined address is FC8E. It is the only register which is 16 bits wide.

The Instruction Register (IR)

The programmer has no access to this register. It holds the *Operation Code* part of the instruction (informing the Control Unit which particular set of actions are to be carried out). (We shall see later that a complete instruction consists of an operation *code* and in most cases an *operand*.)

The Control Unit

When the instruction register contents are received by the control unit it knows exactly what task is to be carried out in order to execute the current instruction.

The first task is to decide whether the complete instruction has been fetched from memory. It already has the Op Code but there may be one or more operands to fetch before the full instruction can be executed. Once the Op Code is decoded (and there is a *different* Op Code for every instruction) the control unit will know how many operands to fetch before it can complete the execution.

The action of the control unit may be divided into two distinct 'phases':

> *The Fetch Phase,* during which the Op Code and operands are read from memory.
> *The Execute Phase,* during which the actual execution of the instruction takes place.

Although the internal logic of the control unit is complex, the actual operations carried out are relatively simple. They consist of opening and closing the input and output gates of a pair of registers one at a time allowing the data in one of them to pass along an internal 'highway' and enter another. Arithmetic processes are automatically processed in the ALU by the simple action of a trigger pulse on the appropriate control line. The complexity arises because all these simple steps must be carried out in the *right order* and at the right time. In fact, what the *program* considers to be a simple 'instruction' is in reality a series of minute steps called the *microprogram* for that particular instruction. These microprograms are stored in a ROM, situated inside the control unit — the Microprogram ROM. (Not to be confused with the external ROM chips.)

Not all instructions take the same time, some taking two clock cycles and other more complex varieties may take up to seven cycles. The 6502 can employ a clock frequency of 1 MHz (one million cycles per second) but the 6502A can operate at 2 MHz. To gain some idea of the time taken to complete an instruction, both fetch and execute phases, a simple addition of the contents of a memory location to the accumulator takes three or four clock cycles depending on its position in RAM. Thus, taking the worst case of four, the 6502 can perform 250 000 additions per second and the 6502A twice this amount.

This completes the details of the 6502 architecture. It is not easy to understand and to those who have never attempted this before it must be bewildering. Fortunately, it is not essential to grasp all these details before proceeding to the next chapter. It may be that when you refer back to it later, it makes more sense.

Remember, if machine code was easy there would be no honour in learning it!

Summary

- *Registers* can be considered as a set of electronic switches which can hold a byte (in some cases two bytes).
- The *accumulator* is the major programmable register and the only one capable of carrying out arithmetic processing.
- The X and Y registers can have their contents swopped with each other or with the accumulator. They can be incremented or decremented for use as counters and are used for a special addressing mode known as *indexed*.
- The *stack pointer* (S) is used to control any part of RAM (in page one) which has been declared the *stack*.

- The stack is a LIFO sytem used for dumping the contents of the other registers.
- The *Processor Status Register* (P) is a set of flag bits which indicate items of interest resulting from the *previous* instruction. The N, V, Z and C bits are used by the control unit to decide whether or not to branch to some out of sequence address.
- The I bit can be used to inhibit an interrrupt request from the peripherals. It can be set or reset under program control.
- The D bit can be set if BCD arithmetic is to be used, otherwise it must be reset by the programmer.
- The currently running program can be interrupted by any one of three signals, IRQ, NMI and RES.
- On receipt of an accepted interrupt, the program diverts to another program called an *interrupt service routine*. On completion of this, the original program is allowed to continue from the point at which it was interrupted.
- IRQ is subject to the I bit in the PSR. NMI and RES ignore the I bit.
- IRQ facilities can be used provided the jump vector in RAM is altered to correspond with your own interrupt service routine. The jump vector will be in RAM at an address which must be looked up in the User's Manual.
- *The Program Counter* (PC), apart from one exception, is not available directly to the programmer. It is automatic in action, always 'pointing' to the address of the next instruction byte. This rhythm is disturbed if the conditions are true in a *branch* type instruction.
- *The Instruction Register* (IR) holds the Op Code part of an instruction while it is being decoded by the control unit. It is not programmable.
- *The Control Unit* contains the set of microprograms necessary to carry out the individual steps required for instruction execution.
- During the *Fetch* phase, the Op Code and operands are read from memory.
- During the *Execute* phase, the instructions are obeyed.
- The number of clock cycles varies with the complexity of the instruction.
- The 6502 operates at a clock frequency of 1 MHz; the 6502A runs twice as quick.
- This chapter may not be digestible in one go!

3

The machine code instruction

Operation codes and operands

The word 'instruction' has been mentioned several times already and we must now discuss it in detail. Superficially, an instruction can be defined as an order given to the 6502 in a form which is directly acceptable to the decode section of the control unit. Unfortunately, this would mean writing a program in the form of a string of depressing '1's and '0's which to any normal human being would be about as stimulating as psychedelic lighting without the flashes. Program writing is made a little 'easier' by persuading the computer to accept machine code instructions either in hexadecimal form via a resident *machine code monitor* or in a slightly higher level form known as an *assembler*. Most home computers have a machine code monitor in ROM but few have a resident assembler although the BBC/Acorn is well equipped in this respect. Whatever method of entry is used, it is essential to grasp the basic format of a computer instruction.

Instruction Format

The list of different instructions which a microprocessor can execute is called the *instruction set*. The 6502 has 56 types of instruction but most of these have thirteen variations on the basic type. Except for a few exceptions, instructions have the following format:

Op Code	Operand

The two parts of a typical instruction are defined as follows:

(a) *The Op Code*
    This is an abbreviation for 'Operation Code' and informs the machine WHAT to do with a data item.
(b) *The Operand*
    This informs the machine WHERE to find the data and is usually the memory ADDRESS which holds it.

27

The Op code is analogous to the verb and the operand to the noun. Consider the sentence:

> Place a copy of the contents of address 35CF into the accumulator.

Using hexadecimal machine code for the 6502, the instruction would be written as:

> AD CF35

The Op Code in hex is the 'AD' part. The operand, also in hex, is the memory address but note this carefully, *written in reverse byte order!* It must be admitted that the previous remark that machine code is made 'easier' if hex is used doesn't seem to be worth much. In defence, this is what it would look like in binary:

> 10101101 1100111100110101

On the other hand if the same instruction was entered by means of a typical assembler it could be written as:

	LDA \$35CF	(operand in hex but right way round)
or	LDA 13775	(operand in decimal)
or perhaps	LDA BLOGS	(symbolic operand)

Before proceeding further, it is wise to spend some time on the details of *assembly* code and the various dielects which are around. Even if your system does not boast an assembler you will find that it is still worth *assuming there is one* while you are developing a program, even if this means a conversion exercise to machine code as a last step before entering the program at the keyboard.

The properties of an Assembler

As assembler is the name for a software system designed to ease the burden of writing machine code programs and to reduce the chance of making errors. It is either resident already in ROM and can be called up by the normal operating system or alternatively it may be available on tape or disk. Assemblers are specific both to the machine and the microprocessor type because it is in reality a software interface between you and the machine code. Unlike the software which is used to enable the use of high level language such as BASIC, each line of a program written in assembly code gives rise only to one line of the equivalent machine coding — a one to one correspondence exists. Thus a program written in assembly code is no shorter in length but it will read more meaningfully to you than the machine code.

Assembler mnemonics

An assembler mnemonic is a three letter group used to replace the Op Code. The letters are standardised by the microprocessor manufacturer and are chosen to represent as far as possible the *meaning* of the Op Code in abbreviated form. The following is an example selection of 6502 Op Codes in their primitive hex form and the equivalent assembler mnemonic:

Op Code in Hex	Mnemonic	Meaning in plain language
AD	LDA	Load accumulator
8D	STA	Store accumulator
AA	TAX	Transfer accumulator to X register
A8	TAY	Transfer accumulator to Y register
8A	TXA	Transfer X register to accumulator
BA	TSX	Transfer Stack pointer to X register
F8	SED	Set decimal mode

The mnemonics, although heavily abbreviated forms, are soon remembered after the first few weeks of use. The hexadecimal Op Code however should never be memorised. Always look it up from the table in Appendix 1. It may take a little of your time but you will find it helpful for future reference to copy out the table and paste it on to card. If you always intend to use the assembler (and if you have one it would be foolish not to) there is of course no need to even know the hex codes and you would find little of interest in the table.

Machine code operands

In machine code, the operand must be given in the form of either a two or four digit hex number which normally represents the address of the data in memory. If the address is in page zero then only two hex digits are required. You will recall that page zero extends from 0000 to 00FF so the first two leading zeros can be omitted. If the address is outside page zero then the full four hex digit address must be given and complicated by an annoying twist:

Remember this: | A 4 hex digit address must be written with the lower order byte first!

29

Example: If the address in hex is actually 35CF, the operand must be written in the form CF35. This is because the 6502 architecture is designed this way round in order to speed up the control cycles. We must remember that machine code is arranged to suit the machine's convenience; humans are considered a nuisance and quite illogical.

Assembly code operands

Assemblers are intended to aid humans in their fight with the machine so we should expect that evils like reverse-byte operands are weeded out. Also the dreaded hex code is replaced by an option allowing the address to be given in normal decimal form. Advanced assemblers even allow you to use *symbolic operands* provided that some previous initialisation has equated the chosen 'symbol' (which could be a group of letters having mnemonic value) to a specific machine address. Symbolic addresses increase the readability of a program and consequently reduce the number of programming errors which might otherwise occur.

Addressing modes

From a practical viewpoint, an addressing *mode* determines what interpretation the machine places on the operand you have written.

To give a quick example, suppose we write LDA 30.

The operand is 30 but does this mean load the *number* 30 into the accumulator or does it mean load the *contents of address* 30 into the accumulator? Some of the instructions can have as many as eight different addressing modes for each one of them. In fact, the power of a microprocessor to process data depends to a great extent on the number of addressing modes for each instruction rather than the number of different instruction forms. The 6502 owes much of its popularity to the number of addressing modes available. There is of course a slight drawback as far as the beginner is concerned — the more addressing modes, the more difficult it is to decide which one to use in a particular case. With practice and confidence however, you will bless rather than curse their availability. In the following attempt to explain some of them we shall stick to the simple LDA as an example mnemonic Op Code but remember that many more instructions allow the same type of addressing modes.

Immediate addressing

With immediate addressing, the operand *is* the data. Memory is not involved. The character used to inform the assembler that the operand is immediate is the symbol # placed before it.

Example: LDA # 30   would load the number 30 into accumulator.

In hex machine code, no special symbol is required because the information is contained in the Op Code itself. Thus in machine code the previous line would be A9 30.

Immediate addressing is used for placing constants in registers.

Zero page addressing

In zero page addressing, the operand is an address in page zero of the required data.

Example   LDA30   would load the contents of address 30 into the accumulator.

In machine code, it would be A5 30.

Page zero is something special and enjoys a higher status than the rest of memory. Wherever possible, page zero should be used because:

(a) the operand only requires one byte of storage
(b) the execution time is reduced

There are also some addressing modes which can only be used in page zero locations. There may be some snags, however, when you try to use page zero because many home computers employ an operating system which purloins most of it. You may have to examine your User's Manual in the section devoted to the contents of page zero with the object of spotting a few empty locations.

Absolute addressing

In absolute addressing, the operand is an address which can be *anywhere* in the 64K memory space (including page zero).

Example: LDA 3056   would load the contents of address 3056 into the accumulator.

The machine code would be AD 5630 (note the reversed bytes).

Note that absolute addressing requires three bytes of storage, one for the Op Code and two for the operand.

Indexed addressing

An *indexed address* is the sum of the operand and the contents of an index register. There are two index registers, X and Y and either can be used. The assembler is informed that indexed addressing is intended by following the operand by a comma and the index X or Y.

Example: LDA 30,X would load into the accumulator the contents of an address effectively equal to *30 + contents of X.*

Thus if X contains 05, the contents of address 35 is loaded; if X contains 06 then contents of address 36 is loaded.

Indexed addressing provides a simple method of using the *same* instruction to refer to *different* addresses by simply changing X (usually by incrementing or decrementing X). A *loop* can be set up as shown in Fig. 3.1, which shows how some particular 'process' can be performed

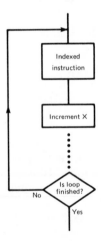

Fig. 3.1. Loop flowchart

on a block of memory addresses. The end-of-loop test will be on the value to which X has grown. Thus if we desire ten revolutions of the loop then if initially X contains 00, the loop must exit when X contains 10.

The following terms are recognised when discussing indexing: The operand of an indexed instruction is called the *base* address, the contents of the index register is called the *relative* address and the sum of the two is called the *effective* address. This relation can be shown as

Effective address = base address + relative address

As an example, in the instruction LDA 60,X assume the X register contains 07. The base address is 60, the relative address is 07 and the effective address is 67.

The 6502 recognises two forms of indexed addressing, as follows.

Zero page indexed addressing

The operand is a single byte, two-hex digit address.

Example: LDA 30,X

In hex machine code,   B5 30
Only the X register can be used in this mode.

Absolute indexed addressing

The operand is a two byte, four-hex digit address.

Example: LDA 4527, X   or   LDA 4527 ,Y

In hex machine code   BD2745   or   B9 2745
Note that either X or Y can be used as the index register.

Indirect addressing

The availability of this mode of addressing raises the status of the 6502, almost approaching that of a minicomputer. In fact the reason that the PET, APPLE, ATOM and ATARI designers chose the 6502 was probably due in some measure to the indirect addressing capability.

Before discussing the details, it would be wise to point out that there are three variants distinguished by the terms *simple indirect, indexed indirect* and *indirect indexed,* all of which are available on the 6502.

Simple indirect addressing

There is only one instruction which can use this mode (actually a jump instruction JMP) but for the moment, we shall continue with the LDA theme purely as an example to illustrate the technique.

Example: LDA (40)   Note the parentheses indicate indirect.

The operand is not the actual address of the data. It is the address of where the address is to be found! Read this again because it is probably gobbledegook the first time — or even the second?

The following illustration may help:

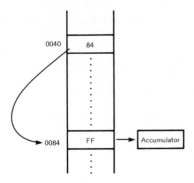

The indirect address is 40 so the machine goes to address 40 first. The contents of 40 (84 in this case) is then interpreted as the *address* of the data so the machine then goes to this address to find the actual data. The data (FF in this case) is then dumped into the accumulator.

An obvious question will arise here; if we wanted to load the contents of address 84 into the accumulator why didn't we just write LDA 84? The advantage of indirect addressing is the ability to *change* the contents of the 'address pointer'. Thus in the above example, the contents of address 40 (the indirect address) contains the address pointer 84 — it is 'pointing' to address 84 where the data lies. If we change this 84 to some other number, the original instruction will fetch data from a different address. Indirect addressing has therefore the same potential for creating loops as the previously discussed indexed addressing but instead of being restricted to X or Y as the variable, a *memory location* can be changed or incremented or decremented. Remember that the description above is based on a fictitious instruction. There is, in fact no 6502 instruction LDA(xx). The real instructions are now discussed.

The indirect address pointer is always two bytes and is stored in two consecutive addresses in the usual awkward order, lower byte first, higher byte second. The only instruction using simple indirect addressing is the jump instruction JMP which is equivalent in BASIC to the GOTO.

Example: JMP (5460) This causes the computer to jump to the indirect address 5460. In address 5460 is the lower order byte of the address pointer; the higher order byte is in 5461.
The hex code is 6C 6054

To illustrate:

JMP (5460)

5460 | 80 |
5461 | 70 |

This would cause the computer to jump to address 7080 for the next instruction. In fact, 7080 would be loaded into the Program Counter. Note that if the address pointer was changed, the jump would be to a different address.

Indexed indirect addressing

This is like indirect addressing but worse! Not only do we have to grasp the essential idea behind indirect addressing, we have to cope with the added complication of indexing at the same time.

The assembler is notified by writing the operand in the form (ZZ,X) so taking the LDA case again for an example and assuming that X contains 05:

LDA (340,X) is the assembly form of the indexed indirect mode. The contents of X are *first added* to the operand to produce 35. This is then taken as the address of the lower order byte of the address pointer, the higher order byte is at address 36 (Fig. 3.2). The operand

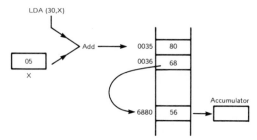

Fig. 3.2. Indexed indirect addressing

is single byte in all indexed indirect instructions, which means the address pointer must be in page zero. If the sum of the operand and X exceeds FF (255 decimal) the carry is ignored and a wrap-around occurs back to address 0000.

One advantage of this mode is the ability to address the entire 64K memory space by the use of a *single* byte operand. The main advantage, however, is the presence of two variable mechanisms, because we can vary X to obtain a new pointer address and the pointer itself can be changed. Thus we can set up looped processes in various blocks of memory under the one indexed indirect instruction. In some textbooks, indexed indirect is called *pre-indexed* indirect.

Finally, on the 6502, only the X register can be used in this mode.

Indirect indexed addressing

This is a kind of mirror image of the previous mode. In the first place, only the Y register can be used to provide indexing. Secondly, the indexed addition is to the address pointer instead of the operand.

The assembler is notified of this mode by writing the operand in the form (ZZ),Y. Be careful to notice the difference between this form and the previous one because they are very similar.

Example: LDA (30),Y   Assume that Y contains 05.

The machine goes to address 30 in which the lower order byte of the address pointer is stored with the higher order byte in 31. The contents of Y is then added to form the effective address pointer (Fig. 3.3).

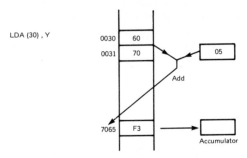

Fig. 3.3. Indexed indirect addressing

Indirect indexed addressing is very useful for processing blocks of data which may be distributed in various pockets throughout the memory space. The address pointer represents the *first* location in the block or list and the Y register can be incremented within the loop. The address pointer then becomes the *base* address, the Y register the *relative* address which together constitutes the *effective* address. To process another block, the mechanism is the same except the address pointer must be changed to point to the start of the new block. Another name for indexed indirect is 'post-indexed'.

Implied addressing

This mode will come as light relief after the previous forms — there is no operand at all. The Op Code itself is sufficient to define the complete instruction. Most of these instructions are concerned with simple register operations such as transfers from one to the other or increments or decrements. It is called implied because the operand is

36

implied rather than specifically stated. (Some texts use the alternative term 'implicit' instead of implied.)

Examples are:

INX	increment X
INY	increment Y
CLC	clear C bit in processor status register
SED	set decimal mode
TAX	transfer accumulator to X
TXA	transfer X to accumulator

Implied addressing is economic because the instruction is only single byte. Another advantage is overcoming deficiencies in the repertoire of some registers. For example, we cannot *add* numbers to the X or Y registers; only the accumulator can perform addition of numbers. If we indeed wish to add, say, 04 to X it is necessary to either use four INX instructions or use a TXA to transfer X to accumulator. We can then add 04 and then use TAX to transfer back again.

Another pair of very economic instructions are concerned with stack operations.

PHA	Push accumulator on stack
PLA	Pull accumulator from stack

Whenever you wish to temporarily store the contents of A, just use PHA. When you want it back again then use PLA. If on the other hand you want to store X or Y temporarily then use TXA or TYA first and then PHA. Remember from previous work that the stack is a LIFO and it will be up to you to keep track of the *order* in which data has been pushed on the stack.

Relative addressing

This form of addressing is used only in conditional branch type instructions. Briefly, the operand signifies *how many bytes* have to be skipped over a program to arrive at the intended destination. For example, the most common branch instruction is BNE ZZ, where BNE means 'branch if not equal' ZZ bytes to obtain the next instruction.

Example: BNE 09 would cause a branch nine bytes forward (if the branch condition was satisfied). If the branch condition was not satisfied, the machine would ignore the instruction and carry on in the normal instruction address sequence.

How about if we wish to branch backwards instead of forwards? In hex machine code this is a bit tricky because backward branches are assumed to be *negative* numbers — and that means two's complement conversion. Thus if we wanted to branch *back* nine bytes we must find the two's complement of 9 as follows:

write down +9 as 00001001, then obtain the two's complement,
                11110111, which in hex is F7.

The instruction would then be BNE F7. (Refer to Chapter 1 if you have forgotten this.)

The mode is called 'relative' addressing because the operand is in essence an offset, relative to the present position.

It is a common source of programming error, particularly in hex machine code, to miscount the bytes by one. This could lead to disastrous results because being one out could mean a branch to an operand and, because of the pathetic intelligence of a computer, would be treated as an Op Code!

The following example may assist in understanding the counting procedure:

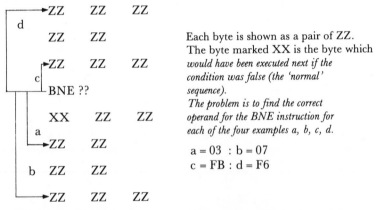

Each byte is shown as a pair of ZZ.
The byte marked XX is the byte which *would have been executed next if the condition was false (the 'normal' sequence).*

The problem is to find the correct operand for the BNE instruction for each of the four examples a, b, c, d.

a = 03 : b = 07
c = FB : d = F6

One outstanding advantage of an assembler is to free the programmer from this error prone procedure. An assembler normally allows you to write a *symbolic label* (of your own choice) to identify the destination byte. The following illustrates:

```
        | BNE BLOGS |
        | ZZ ZZ ZZ  |
BLOGS   | ZZ ZZ     |
```

Since the branch type instructions only have a single byte operand the maximum number of bytes which can be skipped is 127 forward or 128 backwards. (If this is not clear, refer again to Chapter 1.)

If a branch is required outside these limits it is necessary to employ a leap-frogging procedure with the aid of the unconditional jump instruction, JMP. A conditional branch such as BNE can be used for part of the journey as far as the JMP. This will re-route the machine on to the ultimate destination. A jump instruction has a two-byte operand so any part of the memory space can be accessed.

Accumulator addressing

There are a few instructions which can operate on memory locations or the accumulator. They are the shift and rotate instructions which will be treated later.

This concludes the addressing modes available (thirteen in all) and also this chapter. You will continually need to refer to this chapter when in doubt as to the exact significance of a particular mode.

Summary

- A machine code *program* can be entered by a machine code *monitor* which will demand hex code throughout.
- An *assembler* allows easier and less error prone methods of entry.
- All instructions have an Op Code which informs *what* is required.
- Most instructions have an *operand* which supplies information on where to find the required data.
- Some operands are single and some double byte, so a complete instruction in hex code may be one, two or three bytes long.
- Two byte operands if in hex machine code must have the bytes reversed (lower order byte first).
- An assembler accepts the Op Code as three letter mnemonic groups. The operand is assumed to be in decimal. If the dollar sign precedes the operand it indicates hex numbers.
- Some assemblers allow pre-defined symbolic operands.
- The significance attached to an operand defines the *addressing mode*.
- If the operand is the actual data it is called *immediate* mode.
- If the operand is a two-hex digit *address* of the data it is called *page zero* mode (address range 0000 to 00FF).
- If the operand is a four-hex digit address it is called *absolute* addressing (address range 0000 to FFFF).
- Indexed addressing allows the operand address to be modified by the addition of the index register contents.
- In an indexed instruction, the effective address is the sum of the operand and the contents of X (or in some cases Y).

- If the operand is single byte it is *zero page index* mode. Only X allowed.
- If operand is two-byte it is *absolute indexed* and can use X or Y.
- Indirect addressing is when the operand is the address in memory where the *address pointer* is located. An address pointer is the address of the data.
- *Indexed indirect* addressing causes the contents of X to be added to the operand first, the result is the address of the pointer in memory. It is sometimes called pre-indexed addressing. (Remember that only X is allowed.)
- *Indirect indexed* addressing adds the contents of Y to the pointer. It is sometimes called post indexed addressing. (Remember that only Y is allowed.)
- *Implied addressing* does not require an operand. The Op Code is sufficient to define the instruction.
- Register transfers, increments and decrements use implied addressing.
- Accumulator contents can be pushed onto the stack with PHA and recovered with PLA.
- Only branch instructions use *relative addressing*. The operand refers to the number of bytes skipped. Forward branches require a positive operand; backward branches, a negative operand by using the two's complement.
- Branch operands in assembly code can be symbolic labels.
- A branch operand cannot exceed +127 or -128 in decimal (7F or 80 in hex).
- *Accumulator addressing* is an instruction acting only on the accumulator.

4

Classification of instructions

Apart from reference purposes, a list of instructions arranged in alphabetical order is of small value; from a functional viewpoint they would be virtually in random order and consequently would contribute little to the learning process. If however they are arranged in some sort of classified order the task of choosing the right one is made easier, although there will always be arguments as to whether a particular instruction should be under a certain heading or some other. We shall discuss them under the following headings:

(a) Transfers between memory and registers
(b) Transfers between registers
(c) Incrementing and decrementing
(d) Branching and comparisons
(e) Arithmetic and PSR operations
(f) Logical operations
(g) Shifting and rotating
(h) Stack operations.

The information required to completely define the nature of any instruction may be divided into two categories — primary information which *must* be understood first, and secondary information which, although important, can be postponed until needed. One of the features which most of us find bewildering when trying to understand literature written on machine code is the mas of detail surrounding each instruction. For example, the designers of a microprocessor will publish a sheet of paper filled with mind-bending detail on the precise effect of every instruction and its various addressing modes. As an example of scientific condensation it is usually a masterpiece. As a guide to the poor student trying to program for the first time in machine code it is about as informative as a civil service document. Too much information in one place is no information! The number of *clock cycles* required to execute a given instruction may be important to the professional or experienced programmer. On the other hand, a beginner is overjoyed that his program works at all and is unlikely to be concerned about wasting the odd clock cycle. As experience grows, such matters may assume importance but initially they should not be allowed to intrude to the detriment of more pertinent information.

Another characteristic of each instruction which may be considered of secondary importance is the effect on every bit in the Processor Status Register. It is probably sufficient in the initial learning stages to assume that after an instruction, the 'relevant bits in the PSR are updated' and to remember that the *branch* type instructions will *not* affect the PSR in any way; they rely on the PSR information but they leave it alone.

This chapter will be devoted to a coarsely detailed discussion on each instruction.

Transfers between memory and registers

To *transfer* means to place a *copy* of the data in one place (called the *source*) into another place (called the *destination*).

After a transfer, the source information is *preserved* intact; the old information at the destination is *overwritten* by the new.

The direction of transfer is established by the following terms:

To *load* means to transfer from memory to register.

To *store* means to transfer from register to memory.

The 6502 has three load instructions, LDA, LDX and LDY and three store instructions STA, STX and STY. They all set the N and Z bits in the PSR accordingly.

Mnemonic Op Code	Action	Addressing modes supported
LDA	Load accumulator	Immediate / Z page / Absolute / Z page, X / Absolute, X / Absolute, Y / Indexed indirect / Indirect indexed
STA	Store accumulator	As LDA but no immediate mode
LDX	Load X	Immediate / Zero page / Absolute Z page, Y / Absolute, Y
STX	Store X	Z page / Absolute / Z page, Y
LDY	Load Y	Immediate / Z page / Absolute Z page, X / Absolute, X
STY	Store Y	Z page / Absolute / Z page, X

You will notice that immediate addressing can be used with load instructions but not with store instructions. This is because to *store immediate* would demand one operand for the immediate data and a second operand for where it was to be stored — an impossibility in a single-operand computing system. What happens then if we wish to place the constant say, F5 in address 0057? It has to be done in two stages. First load immediate F5 into say, the accumulator (or X or Y) then use a store instruction. The following illustrates:

Assembly code	Hex machine code
LDA #$F5	A9 F5
STA $57	85 57

Transfers between registers

There are four of these: TAX, TAY, TXA, TYA. (There are two others but they are concerned with the stack and will be treated under that heading.) The N and Z bits are set accordingly.

Mnemonic Op Code	Action	Addressing modes supported
TAX	Transfer Accumulator to X	Only implied addressing
TXA	Transfer X to Accumulator	Only implied addressing
TAY	Transfer Accumulator to Y	Only implied addressing
TYA	Transfer Y to Accumulator	Only implied addressing

Register transfers are used mainly to shuffle around data that is in the way but too important to be overwritten.

Incrementing and decrementing

There are four register instructions: DEX, DEY, INX and INY and two memory instructions: DEC and INC. They all set the N and Z bits accordingly.

Mnemonic Op Code	Action	Addressing modes supported
DEX	Decrement X	Only implied addressing
INX	Increment X	Only implied addressing
DEY	Decrement Y	Only implied addressing
INY	Increment Y	Only implied addressing
DEC	Decrement memory contents	Z page / Absolute /
INC	Increment memory contents	Z page, X / Absolute, X

The main use is in loop counting operations, either to count up or down until a certain limit is reached. This can be done in two ways, either by counting up (incrementing) until a certain number is reached or by starting with a number and counting down (decrementing) until zero is reached. For counting up by two or more at a time, consecutive increments can be used or, if the increment is to be large, by using the arithmetic add instruction. Thus if it is required to count X up ten at a time you could use ten consecutive INX lines but it would lack efficiency and elegance. The best way would be to use TXA followed by an add immediate (ten) and then a final TAX. For counts less than five at a time the crude method of multiple INX lines would work out more efficiently.

Branching and comparisons

You will already be familiar with the IF THEN structure of BASIC which is used to program decisions. 'IF such and such is TRUE then perform some action or actions, otherwise do something else'. The ability of a computer to alter the program path depending on certain criteria is the major advantage it has over the simple 'calculator'. We must expect, therefore, that such a facility is inherent within the microprocessor and is not simply a high-level programming gimmick. Unfortunately, although decision branching instructions are inherent in any microprocessor instruction set, they are relatively primitive when compared to the sophisticated doctoring-up versions in a high-level language. For example, in BASIC we take the following line for granted:

100 IF $S + K/2 = S*(K + SIN(D))$ OR $S>G$ THEN $B = J$:
GOTO 450

In machine code this is in the realms of Fantasy. Instruction codes certainly exist for decision making but they are of the naïve 'yes/no' form. Either something happens or it doesn't happen.

In BASIC, exponents seldom use diagrammatic aids to help them in planning their programs; they should do but they don't. In fact, the arrival of the VDU as the primary display device (instead of the early printers or 'teletypes') has in one way encouraged sloppy trial and error programming in BASIC — or indeed other high-level languages. Instead of wasting expensive printer paper to muddle through, the VDU (or TV screen) now tends to be used as a cheap scribbling pad and is quicker to many of us than getting down to serious planning by *flowchart*.

This sloppy method will just not work in machine code unless you are an instinctive coder. Flowcharts are virtually essential in planning a machine code program if it is one which contains multiple decision branches. What is a 'flowchart?'. A flowchart, in the broadest meaning of the term, is a diagrammatic abbreviation for the actual program or rather the *strategy* of it. It is a preliminary statement of the program structure and can be of free form, using any short-cut symbolism which the programmer feels sufficient for the purpose or according to the dictates of established symbolism. If the chart is intended only as a personal aid, then the symbolism employed is unimportant. If, however, the intention is to inform others (as well as yourself) how your masterly program was architectured, it is essential to use formalised symbols or outlines which have the blessing of the Establishment. Some of the most commonly used outlines used in flowcharts are shown in Fig. 4.1.

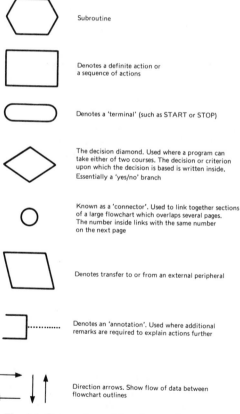

Subroutine

Denotes a definite action or a sequence of actions

Denotes a 'terminal' (such as START or STOP)

The decision diamond. Used where a program can take either of two courses. The decision or criterion upon which the decision is based is written inside. Essentially a 'yes/no' branch

Known as a 'connector'. Used to link together sections of a large flowchart which overlaps several pages. The number inside links with the same number on the next page

Denotes transfer to or from an external peripheral

Denotes an 'annotation'. Used where additional remarks are required to explain actions further

Direction arrows. Show flow of data between flowchart outlines

Fig. 4.1. Commonly used flowchart outlines

A flowchart should not be too detailed and show every step of the program — this would defeat the object and the end result would be as complex as the actual program. A flowchart is strictly a shorthand version so that the overall strategy of the program is clear without polluting the paper with irrelevant or obvious detail. Sometimes it may be desirable to have more than one flowchart, perhaps a very short form first and subsequently another with more detail. The human mind works better if complexity is staged — it objects to detail bulldozed into it without preparation.

The main use of flowcharts is to show the course of decision branches, so the 'diamond' is the most important symbol. A diamond has *one* entry point and *two* exit points, one of them the 'yes' branch and the other the 'no' branch. Most of the coding in this book is of short duration and designed rather as segments which can be used in actual programs, consequently the need for flowcharts to accompany them is minimal. However, when you undertake ambitious programs, flowcharts or some form of strategic planning diagrams will be essential.

There are eight conditional branch instructions in the 6502. They are BNE, BEQ, BPL, BMI, BCC, BCS, BVC and BVS. They all use relative addressing and none of them affect the processor Status Register. If the condition is true (and this knowledge depend on the PSR bits adjusted by the (normally) *immediately previous* instruction, the branch is made. If the conditions are untrue, the branch instruction is ignored and the next sequential instruction is executed. It is essential, when choosing which particular branch instruction is to be used, to be quite certain whether the previous instruction does affect the relevant bits which are being tested.

Mnemonic Op Code	Action	Addressing modes supported
BNE	Branch if not equal $(Z = 0)$	
BEQ	Branch if equal $(Z = 1)$	
BPL	Branch if plus $(N = 0)$	
BMI	Branch if minus $(N = 1)$	Only relative addressing
BCC	Branch if Carry clear $(C = 0)$	
BCS	Branch if Carry set $(C = 1)$	
BVC	Branch if Overflow clear $(V = 0)$	
BVS	Branch if Overflow set $(V = 1)$	

One small point often forgotten is the fact that zero is a *positive* number. Thus if you use BPL you are really testing for 'equal to or greater than zero'. There is no hard and fast rule as to the choice of branch but in general, it is tidier to use the 'yes' branch as a skip (meaning don't do it). For example, if the intention is to increment X *only* if the last result was positive, then the neatest choice of branch is the *opposite*, BMI (Fig. 4.2).

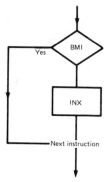

Fig. 4.2. Branch — if loop

Try doing this the other way using BPL and see the kind of ugly mess you get into!

It is time to discuss the comparison instructions. Thus we may want something to happen only if a register contained some particular number. The PSR can only deal with crude results such as whether the number is zero or not zero; it is incapable of informing if the last result was, say, 23 or any other particular number. One way of course is to use the simple mathematical dodge of subtracting the number from the test number and seeing if the result is zero, thus indicating equality. Unfortunately, this operation may corrupt the data merely to test it and may necessitate shuffling around prior and subsequent to the test. To avoid all this trouble the 6502 has three comparison instructions: CMP, CPX and CPY.

One of the primary properties of these instructions is the preservation of the test data. Although the execution involves a subtraction process it is carried out by the microprocessor in a separate pair of registers and the PSR bits are set accordingly. Thus if the two numbers were equal the Z bit would be set to 1. It is worth mentioning that a comparison instruction does absolutely nothing apart from updating the PSR. Unless it is followed immediately by a branch instruction it is a mere passenger.

Mnemonic Op Code	Action	Addressing modes supported
CMP	Compare memory with accumulator (A—M) and set PSR accordingly	Immediate / Z Page / Absolute / Z Page, X / Absolute, X / Absolute Y, / Indirect indexed / Indexed indirect
CPX	Compare memory with X (X—M)	Immediate / Z Page / Absolute
CPY	Compare memory with Y (Y—M)	

It is important in some cases to note that the subtraction test is A–M or X–M or Y–M i.e. the operand data is subtracted *from* the register concerned. Thus if the register contained 5 and the memory data was 6 the comparison instruction would set the N bit to 1, indicating a negative result. If the test is for equality the direction of subtraction is immaterial; if testing for 'greater than' or 'less than' it is vital.

Jump instructions

Jump instructions are similar to branches in as much as they interfere with the normal sequential rhythm of the computer but they are unconditional — they *always* jump. There are only two of these: JMP and JSR.

Mnemonic Op Code	Action	Addressing modes supported
JMP	Jump to the operand address for the next instruction	Absolute Absolute indirect
JSR	Jump to the operand address of the subroutine	Absolute

JMP is straightforward and needs no further comment except to remember once again that if writing in hex machine code, the bytes in the operand must be written back to front, lower order byte first.

JSR however is another matter since it involves some idea of the mechanism of a *subroutine*.

A subroutine is a program segment which may be used more than once. It can be 'called up' by JSR. Thus if a subroutine was located at address 5640 we would write JSR 4056 which would cause a jump to this address for the next instruction. But how do we arrive back to the main program after the subroutine has completed its task?

In the first place, we must remember to always end a subroutine with RTS (which means 'return from subroutine'). The mechanism is as follows:

(a) When JSR is executed, the *return address* is stored on the stack prior to jumping to the subroutine.
(b) On completion of the subroutine, the RTS instruction recovers the return address from the stack and jumps back to this address.

RTS	Return from subroutine	Implied addressing

More detailed treatment of subroutines is dealt with in a later chapter, the only intention at this stage is to explain the mechanism of linkage between main program and subroutine.

Although not strictly a candidate for inclusion under this heading the 'break' instruction BRK does alter the course of a program — in fact it stops it altogether! It is equivalent to STOP or END in BASIC. When writing in hex machine code it is imperative that the end of program should be BRK (hex code 00) otherwise the machine will canter on trying to execute garbage with disastrous results in most cases.

BRK	Break from program (Stop)	Implied addressing

The BRK instruction sets the B bit in the PSR.

The 'bit test'

This is technically a comparison type instruction since it has no other effect except to update the PSR. The full power of the instruction can not be appreciated until we cover the logical AND operation so we shall define it twice; here in a simple but incomplete form and again later.

Mnemonic Op Code	Action	Addressing modes supported
BIT	Examines bit 7 and bit 6 in memory. If bit 7 is 1 then the N bit is set. If bit 6 is 1 then the V bit is set	Z page / Absolute

This is a convenient way of testing whether these two bits are 1 or 0. Bit 7 is of course the sign but and could have been tested by a normal BMI instruction. Bit 6 however has no immediately obvious claim for VIP treatment. However both bit 6 and bit 7 are highly significant as far as the input/output chips are concerned because they are the flags which signal an interrupt request via the IRQ line.

It is important to note that the BIT test does not alter the memory contents or the Accumulator. The remaining details concern the AND mask technique and we shall see that BIT, in addition to the above function, also carries out an AND operation on the Accumulator.

Arithmetic and PSR operations

There are only two arithmetic operations. They perform addition and subtraction of 8-bit binary numbers. However, it is convenient to treat certain other instructions (which affect the Program Status Register) under this heading because of their close association with arithmetic operations. ADC and SBC are for addition and subtraction and CLC, SEC, CLV, SED and CLD are used to set or clear the relevant PSR bits.

Multiplication and division, although taken for granted by humans, are complex operations and the 6502 (and indeed most other 8-bit microprocessors) has no instructions for them. They can however be implemented by 'software' using addition and subtraction.

Mnemonic Op Code	Action	Addressing modes supported
ADC	Add memory to accumulator with carry	Immediate / Z Page / Absolute / Z Page, X / Absolute, X / Absolute Y, / Indexed indirect / Indirect indexed
SBC	Subtract memory from accumulator with carry	
CLC	Clear C bit in PSR	
SEC	Set C bit in PSR	
CLV	Clear V bit in PSR	
SED	Set D bit in PSR (informs that BCD arithmetic is required)	Implied only
CLD	Clear D bit in PSR (informs that normal two's complement arithmetic is required)	

Binary addition

The precise function of ADC can be defined in symbolic terms as follows:

$A = A + M + C$ (M means memory)

If the C bit is clear, the above becomes $A = A + M$
If the C bit is set, the above becomes $A = A + M + 1$

The C bit is set automatically if the result of the addition exceeds FF in unsigned binary (255 in decimal).

The V bit is set automatically to represent *overflow* if the addition exceeds (+127) or (−128) in two's complement binary.

If the precise difference between carry and overflow status is mysterious refer to the paragraph 'The Processor Status Register (P)' in Chapter 2.

If the requirement is limited to addition of single byte numbers having two's complement significance the carry bit is of no importance provided it is reset initially by means of CLC. On the other hand, the overflow bit, V, should be tested after an addition in case the result is invalid.

The C bit however assumes great importance if multibyte numbers are to be added because the correct sum of the higher significant bytes relies on the possibility of a carry from the preceding lower-order byte sum. It is worth emphasising that the C and V bits are only important if the programmer thinks they are!

If for example, the programmer has some idea of the magnitude of the result following an addition process it would be waste of time testing for overflow by the use of the branch BVS. As a further example, if the programmer is treating the numbers as unsigned binary then the V bit will have no significance but the C bit on the other hand now assumes the role of 'overflow detector'.

Binary subtraction

The precise function of SBC which means 'Subtract with carry' can be defined in symbolic terms as follows:

$A = A - M - \overline{C}$

where M is memory and $\overline{C}$ means the carry bit complemented.

When adding (ADC), the carry bit is initially *cleared* by using CLC. When subtracting, the carry bit should be initially *set* by using SEC! Mysterious isn't it? The explanation depends on the maner in which the arithmetic circuits handle subtraction. They use addition of the complement — they add the negative. Thus instead of subtracting, say, 3 from 5, they add (−3) to 5. If there is a carry bit involved it is complemented (if 1 it is changed to 0; if 0 it is changed to 1). Thus if we make sure the carry is *set* before a subtraction, it will be considered by the subtraction circuits to be 'reset'. So, summarising the carry function in both ADC and SBC:

> Clear carry with CLC before starting addition
> Set carry with SEC before starting subtraction

BCD addition and subtraction

If we wish the arithmetic circuitry to consider a byte as two BCD digits we use SED first (Set decimal mode). There is now a drastic change in the carry operations in order to preserve BCD validity. An intermediate carry (sometimes called the 'half-carry' in some texts) comes into play between bit 3 and bit 4 which is acutally the 'boundary' between the two BCD digits.

Example	Normal		Example	BCD addition
9	00001001		9	00001001
add 1	00000001		add 1	00000001
result	00001010		result	00010000

We must remember that the two BCD digits are independent of each other; they are in reality, two entirely separate entities as far as place weightings are concerned. The concept of the half-carry may be understood by considering the two digits separated as follows:

$$0\,0\,0\,0 \quad 1\,0\,0\,1 \qquad \text{(nine in BCD)}$$

bit 4   bit 3

The half-carry action is quite automatic when in BCD mode and the programmer can ignore it. It is however, up to the programmer to ensure that BCD illegals are not allowed in the accumulator, i.e. the six combinations above 1001. In fact, providing that SED is placed at the head of a subtraction or an addition routine, there will be no change required in the program. In case you may be curious how the arithmetic system handles this half-carry, the outline procedure is as follows:

1. Add the two numbers.
2. Is the right hand nibble illegal (greater than 9)?
3. If so, add a further six (which generates the half-carry).

Example:

8	00001000	
add 5	00000101	
result	00001101	illegal
add 6	110	
result	00010011	legal (13 in BCD)

A similar procedure is applied to the left hand nibble, but in this case the carry is the normal C bit status.

It should be mentioned again that BCD format is inherently inefficient; the highest number in a byte is only 99 instead of 255 as in unsigned binary.

Logical operations

The term 'logical' is one of those blanket terms which have a variety of meanings depending on the context in which they are used. As far as we are concerned under this heading,

> A *logic operation* between two bytes simulates the action of eight independent logic *gates*. The two inputs to each gate come from the corresponding bits from each byte.

A logic operation is completely non-arithmetic in nature since there is no carry mechanism from one bit to the next.

The 6502 has three logical instructions AND, ORA and EOR which correspond to the AND, INCLUSIVE-OR and the EXCLUSIVE-OR gates. In case the concept of a logic gate is unfamiliar to you some initial ground work must be covered.

Logic gates

A logic gate has one output, the state of which depends on the combination of the input states. As far as we are concerned, the gates only have two inputs. 'States' of course mean whether a 1 exists or a 0. The definition of the three gates in question is as follows:

(a) The AND — Output is 1 only if *both* are 1.
(b) The INCLUSIVE—OR — Output is 1 if *either* or *both* inputs are 1.
(c) The EXCLUSIVE-OR — Output is 1 only if the two inputs are *different*.

(The INCLUSIVE-OR if often referred to simply as the OR)

Mnemonic Op Code	Action	Addressing modes supported
AND	Performs the logical AND between memory and the Accumulator	Immediate / Z Page / Absolute / Z Page, X / Absolute, X / Absolute Y, / Indexed indirect / Indirect indexed
ORA	Performs the logical INCLUSIVE-OR between memory and the Accumulator	
EOR	Performs the EXCLUSIVE-OR between memory and the Accumulator	

The results of these operations are left in the Accumulator. The obvious question now is, what use are they?

In general, they are used to manipulate certain bits of a word without disturbing the remaining bits — in short, *selective* processing within a byte. When the input/output lines are discussed in a later chapter many uses will be found for switching one particular bit ON or changing the state of another bit. Since the 6502 is a memory-mapped system (see the paragraph 'The input/output chips' in Chapter 1) the eight bits in the memory map location designated as the 'Input/Output Register' are physically connected to the output wires feeding an external system. It may be that one of these wires occupying bit 3 position is indeed the wire which switches on the food mixer! If we wish to switch off the mixer, it would be very awkward if we did this by simply clearing the register — this could switch off the room heater or even the television as well — a ghastly incident if it happened in the middle of *Miss World*. However, it would be easy to selectively switch off the food mixer if we used a suitable logical operation (the AND operation).

The following rules apply to the three logical instructions:

Use AND operation to *clear* selected bits (by using 'zeros' in the mask positions).
Use ORA operation to *set* selected bits (by using 'ones' in the mask positions).
Use EOR operation to *change* selected bits (by using 'ones' in the mask positions).

The term *mask* is used to describe the pattern of bits required in one of the bytes to carry out the selective action on the other byte.

The process is best described with the aid of an example project:

It is required to clear the *three left hand bits* in the Accumulator without altering the remaining bits. How?

From the above rules the AND operation is required and since memory is not involved the mask can be immediate addressing with the pattern 00011111 or 1F hex. The instruction would therefore be

AND #$1F

To investigate, assume the original contents of the accumulator was

11011011	Accumulator originally
00011111	AND mask
00011011	Result in Accumulator

If the bits are examined carefully you will verify that the action between each corresponding pair of bits obeys the AND gate rule. Thus only where there were two '1's before will there be a '1' afterwards. Verify that the five bits on the right are the *same after* as they were before.

As another example, suppose the objective is to set the extreme right and the extreme left bits in the Accumulator to 1 (the msb and the lsb). This time the correct instruction is ORA and the correct mask is 10000001 or 81 hex.

As a final example, suppose the objective is to *change* the state of the third bit from the right (bit 2).

The instruction is EOR and the mask is 00000100 or 04 hex. Thus if bit 2 was originally a '1' then afterwards it would be a '0' (or vice versa). These examples have assumed the mask is in the form of an immediate operand with the data in the Accumulator. Provided that we realise that the result is always in the Accumulator, the relative positions of mask and data is immaterial. Suppose the output register happens to be at address 8004 hex and a device is switched on by bit 5. If we wanted to ensure it was OFF it could be done as follows:

```
LDA# $DF      (DF is the mask 11011111)
AND  $8044
STA  $8004
```

The mask is placed into the Accumulator and the data is ANDed into it. The result (with bit 5 now cleared to 0) is stored back.

The BIT instruction again

The complete description of the BIT instruction (partially described under 'Branching and Comparisons') is now possible. In addition to setting the N and V bits, the AND operation is performed and if the result is zero, the Z bit is set to 1. The formal definition of BIT follows.

Mnemonic Op Code	Action	Addressing modes supported
BIT	Examines bit 7 and bit 6 in memory. If bit 7 is 1 then the N bit is set. If bit 6 is 1 then the V bit is set. *After* this is done, an AND operation is performed on the Accumulator mask and the Z bit is set to 1 if the result of the AND is zero. (Both the Accumulator and memory retain their original contents)	Z page / Absolute

This is a very useful instruction but, obviously from the above, not a very easy one to learn. Some additional remarks may help.

The object of BIT is to test the contents of a memory location for the presence of certain bits without affecting them or the Accumulator in any way. All BIT does is to update the program Status Register.

If the intention is to test the state of bit 6 or bit 7, the contents of the accumulator before the test is unimportant. But if you require knowledge on the state of, say, bit 3 in memory it will be necessary to set the appropriate mask in the accumulator first (by using immediate addressing). If the result of the AND is zero, the Z bit is set.

Example: To test if bit 3 in location 35 is a 1 or a 0.
First load the mask 00001000 into Accumulator   LDA S08
Then BIT test location 35 using Z page addressing   BIT 35

If bit 3 was a '0' the Z bit would be set to 1 and could be found out by the branch instruction BNE or, if required the alternative BEQ. Although it is called a bit *test* we must remember that the complete test must include a subsequent branch instruction. Like the comparison instructions, a bit test not immediately followed by a branch is useless.

Shift and rotate instructions

There are four of these, ASL, LSR, ROL and ROR. Some texts include these under the heading of *logical* instructions because the actions carried out are non-arithmetic in nature.

To *shift* means to push the bit pattern along in one direction as if with a piston. Repeated shifts will eventually push the entire bit pattern out and we can imagine it dropping on the floor — lost for ever!

To *rotate* means to perform a shift action as before but the bits being pushed out at one end are re-inserted at the other again — a kind of circulating bit pattern. In both shift and rotate, the C bit acts as a ninth bit extension of the register or memory.

Mnemonic Op Code	Action	Addressing modes supported
ASL	'Arithmetic' Shift Left Accumulator or memory, using the C bit as the ninth bit at the msb end.	
LSR	'Logical' Shift Right Accumulator or memory, using the C bit as the ninth bit at the lsb end.	Accumulator / Z Page / Z Page, X / Absolute / Absolute, X

ROL   Rotate Left Accumulator or memory, using the C bit as the ninth bit in the loop.

ROR   Rotate Right Accumulator or memory, using the C bit as the ninth bit in the loop.

Arithmetic Shift Left (ASL)

Examples: (a)

	Before	0		1	1	1	1	0	0	0	1
	After ASL	1		1	1	1	0	0	0	1	0

(a)

	Before	1		0	1	1	0	1	1	0	0
	After ASL	0		1	1	0	1	1	0	0	0

Logical Shift Right (LSR)

Examples: (a)

	Before	1	1	1	1	0	0	1	0	0
	After ASL	0	1	1	1	1	0	0	1	0

(a)

	Before	0	0	1	1	0	1	0	1	1
	After ASL	0	0	0	1	1	0	1	0	1

Rotate Left (ROL)

Examples: (a)

	Before	1	0	1	1	1	1	1	1	0
	After ROL	0	1	1	1	1	1	1	0	1

(a)

	Before	0	1	0	1	1	1	1	0	1
	After ROL	1	0	1	1	1	1	0	1	0

Rotate Right (ROR)

Examples: (a)

	Before	1		1	0	0	1	0	1	1	0
	After ROR	0		1	1	0	0	1	0	1	1

(a)

	Before	0		0	1	1	1	1	1	0	0
	After ROR	0		0	0	1	1	1	1	1	0

These examples should be carefully studied before trying to use them. The strangest part of the mechanism is the role of the C bit because of its lofty position up in the Program Status Register. From the mechanism viewpoint however just treat it in the manner described — as a ninth bit in the system. A point of terminology may arise with regard to the two shift instructions. Why is ASL an 'arithmetic' shift left and the LSR a 'logical' shift right? The answer is (probably?) the position of the C bit. With ASL, the C bit occupies the left hand end (which is the msb end) and is the natural position for the carry in an arithmetic protocol. With LSR, the carry is at the right and is therefore unnatural arithmetically and therefore designated as 'logical'.

Employment of shift and rotate instructions demands experience and a certain degree of imagination on the part of the programmer. They can be used in the following circumstances:

Multiplication

If a binary pattern is shifted to the left the effect is multiplication by two. For every shift left the effect is to double the number, subject of course to the limit imposed by an eight bit word.

Example: If 00001010 is given an ASL, it becomes 00010100; the original number was ten and ASL converted it to twenty. If shifted again it becomes forty.

The limit is reached when the carry bit is set; further attempts with ASL would lead to a garbage result. Note that it is not possible to multiply by three or five or any number which is not an integral power of two.

Division

If a binary pattern is shifted to the right, the effect is to divide by two. Every successive LSR will halve the number until bits start being lost again at the right hand end. Since the C bit in LSR is at the right, the presence of a 1 signals the limit is reached. As in multiplication, division is only possible by powers of two.

Positioning bits

Although knowledge of the state of a particular bit can be gained by use of the AND mask technique, shift or rotate instructions can be used to bring the bit of interest into say, the sign position (bit 7). This can then be checked with BMI or BPL. Alternatively, the bit could be brought into the C bit position by LSR. In general, the rotate instructions are 'safer' because the integrity of the bits is preserved — none can drop out of circulation.

When in BCD mode, if a single digit is in the right hand nibble position, four left shifts is equivalent to multiplying by ten:

00001001 after four ASL or four ROL becomes 10010000.
Nine becomes ninety.

Conversion of parallel to serial and vice versa

If a certain 'memory location' is in reality the output register to a peripheral it is sometimes necessary to convert a bit string in the register to a series of bits following one after the other along the same wire, 'parallel to serial conversion'. If say bit 7 is designated the single 'output wire' ASL or ROL can be used to pass the right bits one at a time into the output 'window'. Many peripherals are activated by one wire with the signal bits entering in single file. Suppose the 'peripheral' is an audio amplifier feeding a loudspeaker. The input is a single wire (plus an earth return) and a successive string of bits entering will cause either random noise or a rhythmic beat depending on the bit pattern. A printer is often a serial input device and can be fed by the shift or rotate technique although special chips to handle the conversion are normally used. The reverse case of converting serial inputs to parallel can equally well be done with shift or rotate instructions.

Stack operations

The 'stack' has been mentioned in an earlier chapter but must now be discussed in more detail. You will remember that:

(a) The stack is a certain area in page one of memory (address range 0100 to 01FF); the current address within the stack is defined by the Stack Pointer.
(b) The stack is a LIFO (Last In First Out memory) so the data can only be withdrawn in the inverse order it was stored.

When the microprocessor is first powered up, the content of the stack pointer is unknown — garbage. The first operation is therefore to define the *top* of the stack by loading a number into it. This number is a *pointer* to the stack position in memory. It is normal to load it with FF but because of the extra bit permanently present in the wiring this will cause the stack pointer to hold 1FF (refer to Fig. 2.1). Before proceeding with detail we should be quite certain as to the meaning of 'top' and 'bottom' of the stack because there is a conflict between 'common sense' and pedantry in their application.

The *top* of memory is FFFF. The *bottom* of memory is 0000. The convention is correct, of course (0000 is the lowest address), but because it is natural to number from the top downwards in diagrams and computer programs it is prone to misinterpretation. A reasonable compromise is to use the phrase 'rise towards zero' when considering stack movements because it is awkward to draw the stack the 'correct' way round. Fig. 4.3 shows the portion of the memory map designated

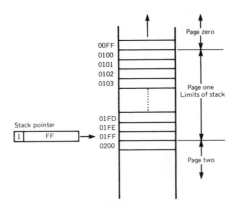

Fig. 4.3. Stack limits in memory and customary starting contents of stack pointer

the 'stack'. The stack pointer is shown as being set to FF (which is of course 1FF) so the first location in the stack which is open for dumping data is 01FF. There is no absolute rule that the stack pointer should be set initially to this position but as data is pushed onto the stack it rises towards zero but cannot rise further than 0100. It is therefore in the interests of maximum stack movement that it should start at the 'bottom'.

There are two instructions TXS and TSX used to transfer data between the Stack Pointer and X and there are four instructions for pushing data on or pulling data off the stack; these are PHA, PLA, PHP, PLP. Only the contents of the Accumulator and PSR can be pushed or pulled from the stack.

Mnemonic Op Code	Action	Addressing modes supported
TXS	Transfer X to Stack Pointer	
TSX	Transfer Stack pointer to X	
PHA	Push Accumulator to stack in address corresponding to the contents of stack pointer. After this, decrement the stack pointer	Implied only
PLA	First increment the stack pointer, then pull from stack into accumulator	
PHP	As PHA above but pushes the Process Status Register instead of the Accumulator	
PLP	As PLA above but pulls the Processor Status Register instead of the Accumulator	

It would appear from study of the above that there is no direct way to set the initial contents of the Stack Pointer. The only way is to set FF in X using immediate addressing and then transfer with TXS.

PHA and PLA are such powerful instructions but so simple to use that they deserve a detailed treatment to supplement the above definitions.

Using PHA

Whenever it is required to temporarily save the contents of the accumulator it is of course always possible to use a normal STA but this will entail supplying the operand address. The advantage of PHA is twofold. Firstly it is an economical *single byte* instruction, and secondly, the programmer is freed from the responsibility of deciding the specific address of the storage location. The action of the stack is quite automatic, rising with each PHA and falling back with each PLA.

To understand the action of PHA, study Fig. 4 which shows the register and memory contents *after* the deed is done. Before the execution, the Stack pointer must have held 01FD so PHA stored the Accumulator contents (35) into the location 01FD. After this, the Stack

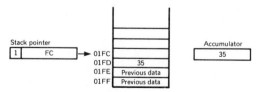

Fig. 4.4. Contents of stack pointer, memory and accumulator immediately after execution of PHA (push accumulator onto stack)

Pointer decremented to 01FC which is the next vacant location (ready for the next PHA).

Using PLA

This is the complementary form used to restore the stack back to the Accumulator (see Fig. 4.5).

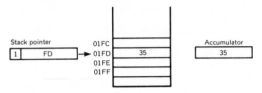

Fig. 4.5. Contents of stack pointer, memory and accumulator immediately after execution of PLA (pull accumulator from stack)

Note carefully that the Stack pointer is *first* decremented before the actual transfer takes place. This is because the pointer is left 'pointing' to an empty location (or one containing garbage) by the previous PHA. There is one snag with stack operations — the information must be drawn from the stack in inverse order to its entrance. It is, after all, a 'last in first out' memory. This restriction is seldom a real handicap because it is used for temporary storage of data. The thing to watch is the order of retrieval.

Example: Suppose we wish to store X, Y and A on the stack by using the transfer instructions as an intermediary. We must push A first, before transferring the remaining registers:

        PHA
        TXA
        PHA
        TYA
        PHA

When it is time to retrieve them, the order must be:

        PLA
        TAY
        PLA
        TAX
        PLA

Use of PHP and PLP

The action of these is identical to PHA and PLA except they act on the

Process Status Register instead of the Accumulator. There are few occasions when it will be necessary to store this register. The exception arises when organising interrupts for it is vital that the status of the system is restored to the prior interrupt form. This will entail the inclusion of the PSR in the list of registers to be dumped to stack.

Use of stack by the microprocessor

The previous treatment of the stack operations has assumed the program has initiated them. Certain stack operations are, however, initiated automatically by the microprogram in the Control ROM. For example, the execution of JSR (Jump to Subroutine) will cause the Program Counter to be dumped on to the stack prior to the actual jump to the subroutine address. Because this register is two bytes long, the stack must rise by two locations to store it. What happens if the subroutine itself uses the stack? This doesn't matter because pushing actions will always be followed eventually by pulling actions within the subroutine, so when it is time to return, the RTS instruction will find the stack in the correct position to restore the Program Counter contents.

This last point illustrates the inherent elegance (almost beauty) of the stack mechanism provided the fundamental rule is observed — *always pull data out in the inverse order of entrance.*

There is one danger ever-present in stack operation, that of overflow! The stack is only 256 bytes in length and it is surprising how easy it is to exceed these limits, particularly if the program is complex with multiple subroutines and interrupts. It is easy to forget that the operating system in a home computer will also be using the stack for its own purposes and which could add an unknown into the situation.

'No operation' instruction (NOP)

NOP does nothing except to increment the Program Counter. It is only a single byte instruction using implied addressing.

What use is it? Its uselessness is its virtue because it provides a one-byte 'hole' in the program. If you are programming in hex machine code it is doubtful if your machine code monitor offers facilities for inserting an extra instruction somewhere in the 'middle'. If you miss one out, you have the gruelling task of re-entering all the bytes downwards in the memory map in order to insert the instruction. This is where the NOP comes in. When developing a program, which almost certainly will mean errors and omissions to attend to, it is a good plan to sprinkle a few NOPs about every ten lines or so — preferably in blocks of three. If you miss an instruction out it is then relatively easy to over-print the NOPs with real instructions after perhaps a bit of juggling.

This concludes the description of the 6502 instruction codes. They are intended only as an introduction and full details, including clock cycles, number of bytes and the hex machine code for each addressing mode are presented in the Appendix. After a time, the contents of this chapter will seldom be consulted and you as a programmer will work almost entirely from the condensed form in Appendix A.

Summary

- During a transfer, the *source* is left intact but the *destination* is overwritten by the new contents.
- Incrementing means to add 1; decrementing means to subtract 1.
- All branch-type instructions use *relative* addressing.
- The branch takes place depending on the relevant bits set in the PSR which were established by the *preceding* instruction result. If the branch *conditions* are not fulfilled, the machine carries on normally without branching.
- *Compare* instructions perform a substraction between memory and Acc but restore the original contents afterwards. Their only action is to update the PSR. They are only of use if followed by a Branch instruction.
- *Jump* instructions are really *unconditional* branches — they always branch.
- To use a subroutine, the calling procedure is JSR followed by the absolute address. To return from a subroutine, its last instruction must be RTS.
- To stop a program use BRK (break).
- The BIT instruction transfers bit 6 and 7 of the tested location into the V and N bits respectively. It then carries out a logical AND, using the Acc as the mask, and sets the Z bit if the result is zero. The original memory location is left intact.
- The only instruction for adding into the Acc is ADC which takes the carry bit (C) into consideration. Before starting an addition process the C bit must be cleared by using CLC.
- To subtract from the Acc use SBC, which again takes the C bit into consideration. Because subtraction is carried out by complementary addition, the C bit should be *set to 1* first.

- To add and subtract BCD numbers use SED first but remember to use CLD before reverting to normal binary arithmetic.
- There are three *logical* instructions AND, ORA and EOR.
- AND is used to *clear* selected bits, ORA is used to *set* selected bits and EOR is used to *change* selected bits.
- There are two shift instructions, ASL for shifting left and LSR for shifting right. The C bit acts as a ninth bit extension.
- There are two rotate instructions, ROL for rotating left and ROR for rotating right. The C bit is included within the 'loop'.
- The Stack is a programmably designated area in page one of memory. The Stack Pointer contents always point to the address of the current stack location.
- PHA pushes the Acc onto the stack then moves the stack pointer contents *up one towards zero*.
- PLA moves the contents of the Stack Pointer *down one away from zero* then transfers the stack contents back to the Acc.
- The PSR can be pushed and pulled by the use of PHP and PLP respectively.
- Always retrieve data from the stack in inverse order of storage.
- The stack is only 255 bytes long and could overflow.
- NOP is useful for sprinkling holes in a program in case you want to fill them later.

5

Applying the instruction set

Preliminary advice

It is one thing knowing *what* each instruction will do. It is quite another matter choosing which one to use and in what *order* they should be used to implement a given programming objective. This is the primary division between knowledge and the application of knowledge — it is in fact the *art* of programming. These remarks apply equally to BASIC and machine language but have a greater relevance to the latter. With due respects to Dijkstra, it is an art — not a *science*. Perhaps the soundest advice to the newcomer to machine code is the old adage, 'don't run until you can walk'. Try very simple objectives first and ignore the scorn of your colleagues who are hooked on BASIC. The typical irritating remark which you must accustom yourself to ignore is "Is that *all* it does? I can do that in two lines in BASIC." In a few months, they may be coming to you for advice on how to make their tank, missile or other graphical contraption 'move across the screen quicker'.

Importance of the User's Manual

Whichever machine you own, the resident operating system and the BASIC interpreter will make considerable demands on the available address space. In particular, much of the valuable page zero will have probably been pilfered by these systems. If you later intend to write programs completely in machine code then it is probably allowable to occupy these hallowed places subject to the requirements of the machine code monitor. Apart from the restrictions on use of page zero, you cannot use any part of RAM without consulting the User's Manual supplied with your machine. From this, you will learn the upper and lower address limits and how it is utilised. Study of this will reveal (perhaps?) the areas of memory which are vacant and suitable for inclusion of your machine code programs or subroutines. There may be for example, an area dedicated to the servicing of some peripheral which you don't have. This would be an ideal area, safe from the ravages of BASIC. Those of you who own Commodore PETs will know that the RAM area reserved for the second cassette buffer (few people ever bother with the second cassette) covers an area of 192 bytes from address 033A hex onwards. In case you think that 192 bytes is a paltry amount of memory you will probably find it more than ample for the programs which you are likely to manage in the early stages. Subroutines of 20 or 30 bytes can be surprisingly powerful — remember that machine code is very economical in memory use.

If you do require a substantial amount of RAM for your program it is possible to restrict the boundaries of the BASIC text by use of HIMEM or LOWMEM (if you have them) or by a suitable POKE instruction into the relevant pointer. Again, this knowledge must be gleaned from the User's Manual.

Program and data requirements

It is important to distinguish between the program and the data to which the program refers. The program bytes must occupy consecutive bytes in memory but the data bytes can be sprinkled anywhere provided that certain rules, dictated by the addressing mode, are preserved. Thus an *instruction* using zero-page addressing doesn't itself have to be in page zero although the data byte at the operand address must be. As mentioned before, the majority of page zero is normally occupied although there are a few holes. These must be considered as treasure trove once they have been prised out from the Manual. If you use indexed indirect or indirect indexed addressing you will need to examine page zero to find a pair of adjacent locations to hold the address pointer.

Machine code or assembly code?

At the time of writing, very few home computers arrive with a resident assembler although most include a machine code Monitor for entering a program in hex. There is of course no contest between the two. If you have an assembler then let the machine code monitor hibernate in its ROM. Whether you write in hex or assembly code it is *still machine code* as far as the microprocessor is concerned. The advantage of an assembler is the facility it offers for entering machine code in more civilised notation and therefore in less error prone form.

Assembler notation

All assemblers share certain common properties and much of the notation is standardised but unfortunately not all of it! In the example programs, the notation used is

Mnemonic Op code	Three letter goup as in APPENDIX A
Immediate addressing	#
Operands in decimal	assumed unless prefixed by $
Operands in hex	$
Symbolic operands	free choice (not more than five letters)

Although when entering hex machine code the operands must be written 'back to front' (if double byte) this does not apply in assembly code.

Example: In assembly operands the absolute address 0640 is written 0640. In hex machine code, it must be written 40 60.

Assembler addressing modes

With hex machine code, there is a different Op Code for each addressing mode so there is no need to indicate to the monitor *which* mode is intended. With an assembler however, it is necessary to use the exact symbolism for the operand.
  In the examples which follow, the symbolism used is:

ZERO PAGE	ZZZ	HH	
ABSOLUTE	ZZZ	HHHH	
ZERO PAGED INDEXED	ZZZ	HH, X	(or HH, Y)
ABSOLUTE INDEXED	ZZZ	HHHH, X	(or HHHH, Y)
INDEXED INDIRECT	ZZZ	(HH, X)	
INDIRECT INDEXED	ZZZ	(HH), Y	

Note: ZZZ is the Op Code mnemonic
      HH is a single byte operand
      HHHH is a double byte operand

Sample layout of program

The actual 'program' has no particular purpose except to illustrate simple operations involving transfers between registers, adding and stack transfers.

Assembly code		Remarks		Hex code	
LDX	# $FF	FF → X	0340	A2	FF
TXS		Transfer X to SP	2	9A	
LDA	# $65	65 → Acc	3	A9	65
PHA		Push Acc on stack	5	48	
ADC	# $01	Add 1 to Acc	6	69	01
PHA		Push Acc on stack	8	48	
PLA		Pull from stack to Acc	9	68	
TAX		Acc → X	A	AA	
PLA		Pull from stack to Acc	B	68	
TAY		Acc → Y	C	A8	
BRK		Stop	D	00	

After this is run, the register contents are

PC	Acc	X	Y	SP
034E	65	66	65	FF

Assuming the hex code above was entered via a Machine Code Monitor, such as on the PET, the procedure would be:

(a) Decide where to store the program (assume address 0340 onwards).

(b) Display a block of bytes from memory by keying M 0340, 0350.

(c) Using the cursor, overwrite the bytes of the program.

The display would appear as follows:

0340	A2	FF	9A	A9	65	48	69	01
0348	48	68	AA	68	A8	00	/ /	/ /
0350	/ /	/ /	/ /	/ /	/ /	/ /	/ /	/ /

The leftmost column is the hex address of the first byte of each row. The program ends at 00 (BRK), the 6th byte on row two; the slashes indicate garbage bytes.

You would be well advised to study the layout carefully, particularly the translation from the assembly code to the hex code. This will require continual reference to the Machine Code Summary (Appendix A). It should be stressed that the procedure for entering machine code or the assembler notation may not be the same in your machine. For example, the *remarks* column shown can actually be entered alongside the assembly code in most assemblers, usually prefixed by a semicolon (;).

Short program examples

These examples may be helpful in getting the feel of machine code. They gradually increase in difficulty as more of the instructions are introduced. The programs in themselves are not particularly useful but the ideas may help in building up confidence so you should enter them all and satisfy yourself they work. The *remarks* column is only used where the particular coding is obscure. In assembly code, symbolic operands have been used in BRANCH type instructions with the destination line prefixed by the symbolised form in the 'label' field.

Program 1. Add contents of address 0360 and 0361 and store result in address 0362

CLC		Clear carry bit	18		
LDA	# $00	Clear Acc	A9	00	
ADC	$0360		6D	60	03
ADC	$0361		6D	61	03
STA	$0362	Store result	8D	62	03
BRK			00		

Before running, enter the numbers to be added into the two locations. Then try the program with several different numbers, including mixed signs.

Program 2. Load X with 3,Y with 5. Add them up and store result in 0360

CLC			18		
LDX	# $03		A2	03	
LDY	# $05		A0	05	
STX	$0360	Use 0360 as temporary store	8E	60	03
TYA			98		
ADC	$0360	Add original contents of X	6D	60	03
STA	$0360	Store result back	8D	60	03
BRK					

Note the shuffling around required to add X to Y (has to be done via the Acc).

Program 3. Swop over contents of 0360 and 0361

LDA	$0360	Load 1st number into Acc	AD	60	03
LDX	$0361	Load 2nd number into X	AE	61	03
STA	$0361		8D	61	03
STX	$0360		8E	60	03
BRK			00		

Program 4. Examine location 0360. If it contains a positive number, load FF into X. If it contains a negative number, load EE into X

	LDA	$0360		AD 60	03
	BMI	NEG		30	03
	LDX	#$FF		A2	FF
	BRK		Stops here if positive	00	
NEG	LDX	#$EE		A2	EE
	BRK		Stops here if negative	00	

Remember the largest positive number is 01111111 = 7F hex. Try out with different pairs of numbers. To test overflow try 7F + 01 which gives the 'correct' answer 80 if interpreted as unsigned binary but as far as two's complement is concerned, it is a false answer; the V bit is set.

Program 5. Add up the contents of locations 0360 and 0361 and store result in 0362. If overflow is caused, Load FF into Y

	LDY	#$00		A0 00	
	CLC			18	
	LDA	$0360	Load 1st number	AD 60	03
	ADC	$0361	Add 2nd number	6D 61	03
	BVC	OK	Branch if clear to label 'OK'	50 02	
	LDY	#$FF	Overflow status	A0 FF	
OK	STA	$0362	Store result	8D 62	03
	BRK			00	

Program 6. Assume two numbers are in locations 0360 and 0361. If the smaller number is in 0361, swop them over

	LDA	$0361	Examine the first number	AD 61	03
	CMP	$0360	Compare it with the second	CD 60	03
	BMI	SWOP		30	01
	BRK		Stop here if correct	00	
SWOP	TAX			AA	
	LDA	$0360		AD 60	03
	STA	$0361		8D 61	03
	STX	$0360		8E 60	03
	BRK		Stop here after swopping	00	

Program 7. Store the integers 0, 1, 2, . . . 9 in addresses 0360 . . . 0369

	LDX	#$00	Clear index register	A2 00	
	LDA	#$00	Clear Acc	A9 00	
STORE	STA	$0360, X	Store Acc in (0360 + X)	9D 60	03
	INX		Increment X	E8	
	TXA		Effectively increment Acc	8A	
	CPX	#$0A	Ten jobs to do!	E0 0A	
	BNE	STORE	Go back if X not yet ten	D0 F7	
	BRK		All jobs done	00	

Study Program 7 carefully because it is the first example on the use of indexed addressing in creating a loop. It conforms in principle to the general purpose flowchart of Fig. 5.1.

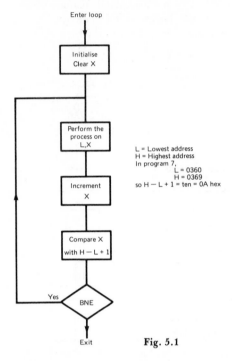

L = Lowest address
H = Highest address
In program 7,
$\qquad$ L = 0360
$\qquad$ H = 0369
so H − L + 1 = ten = 0A hex

Fig. 5.1

There are numerous occasions when a certain *process* must be performed on consecutive locations in memory and the flowchart provides a general guide on choosing the loop constants. Note the process is first performed on the *lowest address* (the base address) and the index is *increased* each time round the loop until the limit is reached. In Program 7, this limit is when the value in X has grown to ten (the total number of jobs to be done). In fact the equation H–L + 1 is indeed equal to the total number of jobs to be done.

To illustrate how program 7 can be modified, suppose the objective was changed to:

Store the integers 0,1,2, — n in addresses 0350 to 0385 hex.

The program would remain the same except the third line would be,

LDA 0350,X

and the comparison line would be CPX # $36 (0385–0350 + 1).

There is an alternative method of attack in which the process is carried out in reverse order, 'last' address first. The index register is first loaded with the 'number of jobs to be done' (H–L + 1) and decremented until zero is reached. This method avoids using a CMP instruction since the BNE itself can test for zero in X. The operand of the indexed instruction, however, must be L–1 which is a bit awkward to remember. The next program uses this method.

Program 8. Clear the addresses 0360 . . . 0369 (see Fig. 5.2)

	LDX	#$0A	Number of jobs	A2	0A	
	LDA	#$00	Clear Acc	A9	00	
BACK	STA	$035F, X	Store Acc in L—1, X	9D	5F	03
	DEX		Decrement X	CA		
	BNE BACK		Branch back if X not yet zero	D0	FA	
	BRK		All jobs done	00		

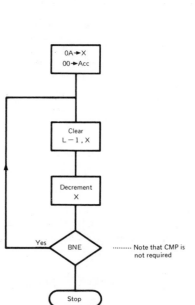

Fig. 5.2. Flowchart for program 8

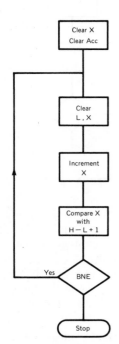

Fig. 5.3. Program 8 if counting up method used

To illustrate the 'counting up' method, examine Fig. 5.3, which shows how Program 8 would be arranged.

Program 9. Search the addresses 0360 . . . 0380 for the number of time the pattern FF is stored. Place answer in 0381

	LDX	# $00	Clear X	A2	00	
	STX	$0381	Clear address holding answer	8E	81	03
BACK	LDA	$0360, X	Load contents of (0360 + X)	BD	60	03
	CMP	# $FF	Compare with pattern FF	C9	FF	
	BNE	SKIP	No pattern in this address	D0	03	
	INC	$0381	Pattern found so add 1 to answer	EE	81	03
SKIP	INX		Increment X	E8		
	CPX	# $21	All jobs done?	E0	21	
	BNE	BACK	No	D0	F1	
	BRK		Yes	00		

Program 10. Search page zero from 00 to F2 for the first occurrence of the pattern AA. When found, place the ADDRESS in which it was found in 0360. If not found at all leave FF in 0360

	LDX	# $00	Clear X	A2	00	
	LDA	# $FF	'Not found' in pattern in Acc	A9	FF	
	STA	$0360	Store it	8D	60	03
BACK	LDA	$00, X	Load contents of (00 + X)	B5	00	
	CPM	# $AA	Compare with pattern AA	C9	AA	
	BEQ	FOUND	Pattern found	F0	06	
	INX		Increment X	E8		
	CPX	# $F3	All jobs done	E0	F3	
	BNE	BACK	No	D0	F5	
	BRK		Stop here if pattern not found	00		
FOUND	STX	$0360	X contains the address	8E	60	03
	BRK		Stop here if pattern found	00		

The problem of knowing *where* a certain item is stored is often as important as knowing *what* item is stored. The address is often more important than the contents. Program 10 illustrates how the index register contents give a clue as to the address although, since the search was from address 00 to F2, it was more than a clue because X *was* the address. In the more general case, the address of the found item can be obtained by adding X to the base address; the base address being the operand (L in the flowcharts).

As an example, suppose the objective of Program 10 was changed to read 'Search page zero from 24 to FF —', the found item would have an address equal to 24 + X. If it was found immediately at the head of the list, X would still be at zero so the address would be 24 + 0 or 24! If it was found at the next address, X would have grown to 1 so again the result is valid (24 + X).

Program 11. A block of addresses 0360 to 0369 is storing numbers in two's complement form. Add up the numbers and store total in 0370

	CLC		Clear Carry bit	18
	LDX	#$00	Clear X	A2 00
	TXA		Clear A as well	8A
BACK	ADC	$0360, X	Add contents of (0360 + X)	7D 60 03
	INX		Increment X	E8
	CPX	#$0A	All jobs done?	E0 0A
	BNE	BACK	No	D0 F8
	STA	$0370	Yes so store total	8D 70 03
	BRK		Stop	00

No provision is made for detecting overflow but the extra lines would be similar to those in Program 5.

Program 12. A list of data items is stored in 0360 to 0370. Relocate this data into 0380 to 0390

	LDX	#$00	Clear X	A2
BACK	LDA	$0360, X	Load contents of old address	BD 60 03
	STA	$0380, Y	Store in new address	9D 80 03
	INX		Increment X	E8
	CPX	#$11	All jobs done?	E0 11
	BNE	BACK	No	D0 F5
	BRK		Yes	00

The method shown to relocate is fairly straightforward but only because the new address block was not overlapping the old. If the objective was altered to say — relocate from 0360—0370 to the new block 0365 — 0375, the above scheme would not work because the relocation loop would erase data before it was relocated. The next program will illustrate the alternative procedures.

Program 13. A list of data items is stored in 0360 . . . 0370. Relocate in 0365 . . . 0375

	LDX	#$11	Number of jobs	A2 11
BACK	LDA	$035F, X	Load L–1, X (old location)	BD 5F 03
	STA	$0364, X	Store L–1, X (new location)	9D 64 03
	DEX		Decrement X	CA
	BNE	BACK	All jobs done?	D0 F7
	BRK		Yes	00

The relocation in this program takes place bottom upwards (similar to the technique employed in Program 8) so avoiding premature erasure of data. The first address to be actioned will be 0370 (the last address in the original block), the data being transferred to 0375 (the last address in the new block).

Program 14. Time delay proportional to N time units, where N is the contents of 0360

LDX	$0360	Load N	AE	60	03
DEX		Decrement	CA		
BNE	TIME	Not yet zero	D0	FD	
BRK		Delay expired	00		

Delays are often required, especially when controlling peripherals. The standard method is based on the above and consists of starting with a number N and counting it down until zero is reached. The actual delay depends on the value of N and also the microprocessor clock. The delay loop is over two instructions, DEX and BNE. Referring to Appendix A, it will be noted that these instructions take two clock cycles each.

Example: Assume the clock frequency is 1 MHz (one million cycles per sec), then each cycle is 1 μs (microsecond) and one loop cycle would be 4μs. Thus if N was FF (which is 255 in decimal), the time delay would be $255 \times 4 = 1024\mu$s which is just over a millisecond. This would be the maximum possible delay with such a simple program. As far as a human is concerned, this would be an undetectable delay, although for handling 'slow' peripherals it could very well be more than adequate.

If longer delays are required it is possible to have a loop within a loop, similar to nested FOR loops in BASIC. Obviously, the program above which breaks (BRK) out after the expired time would have little practical value but, if BRK is changed to RTS, the program can be used as a subroutine. The practice of using computer instructions to produce a delay could cause trouble in some systems. If for example, a program allows interrupts to occur within a timing loop the effect could be serious. Most microcomputer systems now employ Input/Output chips which provide sophisticated functions such as an independent timer. This allows the time delay to be considered an external hardware, rather than software, problem.

Program 15. Double loop time delay subroutine. Number N in Acc determines the delay.
If Acc arrives with FF, the inner loop will revolve 255 times for every revolution of the outer loop. Total delay thus depends on $255 \times 255 = 65\,000$ rev (approx) (see Fig. 5.4)

	TAY		Y now holds N	A8	
LOOP 2	TAX		So does X	AA	
LOOP 1	DEX		Inner loop decrement	CA	
	BNE	LOOP 1	Bottom of inner loop	DO	FD
	DEY		Outer loop decrement	88	
	BNE	LOOP 2	Bottom of outer loop	DO	F9
	RTS		Delay completed	60	

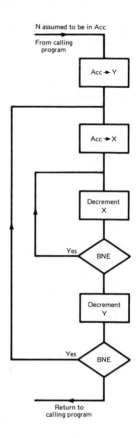

N assumed to be in Acc

From calling program

Acc → Y

Acc → X

Decrement X

BNE — Yes

Decrement Y

BNE — Yes

Return to calling program

Fig. 5.4. Double delay loop

Program 16. Load Acc with the number 77 and store this in address 0360 using Indirect Indexed mode. The indirect address locations to be 06 and 07 in page zero

LDY	#$00	Clear Y	A0	00
LDA	#$60		A9	60
STA	06	Set indirect address in	85	06
LDA	#$03	page zero	A9	03
STA	07		85	07
LDA	#$77	Load the number 77 into Acc	A9	77
STA	(06),Y	Store in 0360 (via pointer)	91	06
BRK			00	

This program is easy to criticise — what a long way round just to store 77 in address 0360! In defence, the intention is simply to get the feel of indirect addressing before progressing to more involved actions. Index register Y is cleared first so as to minimise the complexity and reduce

77

the mode to 'simple indirect'. Remember that Indirect Indexed mode uses the Y register to modify the address pointer. Fig. 5.5 may help in understanding the program.

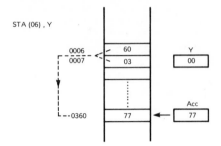

Fig. 5.5. Idea behind program 16

The contents of 0006 and 0007 are the lower and higher order bytes respectively of the address pointer.

Warning: Remember that page zero locations are sacrosanct and in some micros using 06 and 07 could cause trouble. Consult your manual on this point.

Program 17. Store the integers 0, 1, 2 . . . 9 in the addresses 0360 to 0369 using Indirect Indexed mode. The indirect address locations to be 06 and 07 in page zero

	LDY	#$00	Clear Y	A0	00
	LDA	#$60		A9	60
	STA	06	Set indirect address in	85	06
	LDA	#$03	page zero	A9	03
	STA	07		85	07
BACK	TYA		Transfer Y to Acc	98	
	STA	(06),Y	Store in (pointed address + Y)	91	06
	INY		Increment Y	C8	
	CPX	#$OA	All integers stored?	CO	OA
	BNE	BACK	No	DO	F8
	BRK		Yes	00	

The first five instructions are identical to those of Program 16 and are simply to set the address pointer.

The remaining instructions increment Y in a loop until it grows to OA (ten jobs). Since it uses Indirect Indexed by Y, the effective address is increased each time. Thus, when Y has grown to 03, the effective address is 0360 + 03. Although this program does a little more than the previous one, it may still appear to be a roundabout method. The point

78

to appreciate, however, is that a change in the contents of the address pointer (06 and 07) would cause the same program to store the integers in an entirely different address block.

Program 18. Using Indexed Indirect mode, store the ASCII code for 'space' in all locations from 8000 onwards, covering a range of four complete pages. Use addresses 06 and 07 in page zero for pointer

	LDX	#$00		A2	00
	TXA		Clear X, A and Y	8A	
	TAY			A8	
	STA	06		85	06
	LDA	#$80	Set indirect address	A9	80
	STA	07	in page zero	85	07
	LDA	#$20	Load Acc with 20 (ASCII code)	A9	20
BACK	STA	(06),Y	Store Acc in pointed address + Y	91	06
	INY			C8	
	CPY	#$00	Repeat for complete page	C0	00
	BNE	BACK		D0	F9
	INX		Increment X	E8	
	INC	07	Increment high byte of pointer	E6	07
	LDY	#$00	Reset Y for start of next page	A0	00
	CPX	#$04	Pages finished ?	E0	04
	BNE	BACK	No	D0	F0
	BRK		Yes	00	

This program is worth studying with great care, not because it is a particularly efficient way to achieve the objective, but because it forms a good exercise in the concept of *page boundaries* as well as indirect indexed addressing. As in previous examples, the address pointer is in 06 and 07. The lower order byte of the address (in 06) is indexed by Y each time until it has grown to FF which is the last location on a page. To repeat the procedure on the next page, Y is reset to zero and the *higher* byte of the pointer is incremented. Remember from earlier work on the concept of a 'page' that the higher order byte is the page number and the lower order byte is the address within that page. Note that the test for the end of page is CPY #$00 and not CPY #$FF. This is due to the preceding INY which increments FF to 00 (FF is −1 so incrementing by + 1 yields 00).

The fourth line from the bottom, LDY #$00, is not really necessary (because Y would already have been zero at this point in the program) but it aids comprehension. As an exercise, replace the line with two NOPs, OP code EA, and prove that it still works OK.

The program indicates how the screen could be painted with characters. If we assume the screen RAM locations start from 8000 hex and occupy *exactly* four pages (1K) this program would clear the screen by printing spaces in every position. The PET screen is almost identical, except that only 1000 character positions are available. For any computer which has a memory mapped screen, the pointer in addresses 06 and 07 would have to be changed to suit the screen starting address. To paint a character on the screen it is normally sufficient to look up the ASCII code (refer to Appendix 2) although not all computers stick rigidly to the standard.

One of the difficulties which beset the newcomer to machine code is the limit of 255 decimal imposed by the 6502 8-bit registers. Thus it is not possible to use indexed addressing to cover the entire screen area. The previous program used indirect addressing with Y as an index to cover one page and X as a simple counter to 'turn the pages'. An alternative method would be to retain indirect addressing and increment the pointer or use the ADC 01. Unfortunately, the same problem arises — we can't add or increment to a final value greater than 255 decimal — or can we? The answer is to use *double-precision* addition, or if that is not enough, treble-precision. This will be one of the techniques discussed in the next chapter.

Summary

- Practise on very simple programs until confidence is gained.
- Before attempting to enter machine code, consult the User's Manual to establish *where* you can safely enter it.
- A program will be a number of bytes occupying contiguous addresses.
- There is no rule regarding the location of the data bytes; they can be scattered.
- Page zero is special. Free locations are difficult to find because the BASIC system uses most of the area.
- Indirect addressing require the pointers to be stored in page zero.
- Machine code programs can be entered in a more friendly manner if assembly code is used. If your system does not have an assembler you must write in hexadecimal machine code.
- In hex machine code, you must look up Appendix 1 to obtain the Op Code.
- There is a different hex code for each addressing mode.
- In Assembly code, the same mnemonic three-letter group is used, irrespective of the addressing mode. The Assembler is notified of the mode by the symbols and punctuation used with the operand address.
- Double byte operands of hex coding must be written 'backwards', *lower order* byte of address *first*.

- In Assembly code, the operand can be stated in terms of decimal, hex or in some assemblers even in binary — provided that the prefix symbol notifies the assembler in the prescribed manner.
- A loop which operates on consecutive locations in memory can be implemented by the use of indexed addressing.
- A loop begins with *initialisation* in order to establish the starting condition of the index register or in some cases, the Accumulator.
- Within the loop is the *process* which is performed on the memory locations via indexed addressing mode.
- The index register is incremented (or in some cases, decremented) to prepare for the next revolution of the loop.
- The bottom of the loop contains the 'end of job' test.
- If the index register starts at zero and is *incremented*, the end of job test is a Compare (CPX), (CPY) or in some cases (CMP) followed by a BNE.
- If a search is conducted to discover the presence of a certain data pattern, the *address* of the data can be found by adding the base address (the operand usually) to the current index register contents.
- Relocating programs or data can be performed by indexed loop but care must be taken not to erase any of the source data by overwriting the destination data. This can occur if there is overlap between source and destination.
- Delays can be interposed within a program by simple loops which count a number down to zero. The delay time depends on the number and the cycle time of the instructions within the loop.
- Delays more than a few milliseconds require nested loops.
- Indirect addressing enables any address in the 64K memory space to be accessed by a single byte operand.
- The effective address can be changed by the index register and the memory contents of the pointer.

6

Arithmetical and logical manipulations

Although many of the previous programming examples have involved simple addition and subtraction there has been little attention paid to the detailed mechanism of two's complement arithmetic. It is useful to understand the procedures if only to increase confidence in their use. For example, how does the microprocessor distinguish between a *carry* and an *overflow* situation? Is it possible to use an ADC instruction to *subtract* or must we always use SBC? Why do we have to *clear* the carry before ADC but *set* the carry before SBC? How can *large* numbers be added together in spite of the limitations imposed by an eight-bit word length? Partial answers have been given to some of these questions in earlier chapters but it is time to attack them with more vigour.

Single-byte addition

Study the following examples, particularly the final state of the C and V bits.

---

1. Add (+ 5) to (+ 5)

| | 00000101 | + 5 | Accumulator |
| | 00000101 | + 5 | Operand data |

$0 \leftarrow$ 00001010   + 10   Accumulator result

Note the carry out was a '0' (no carry !)
There was no overflow so the V bit is '0'.

---

2. Add (−5) to (+ 5)

| | 00000101 | + 5 | Accumulator |
| | 11111011 | −5 | Operand data |

$1 \leftarrow$ 00000000   0   Accumulator result

This time the carry is '1' but still no overflow.

It would seem from the above example that we can have a correct answer in two's complement even if there is a carry '1' out.

3. Add (−5) to (+ 3)		00000011	+ 3	Accumulator
		11111011	−5	Operand data
	0	11111110	−2	Accumulator result

Carry out '0' and no overflow.

No carry this time, the Accumulator sign bit *changed* but still the answer was correct and no overflow exists. It would seem therefore that a mere change of sign bit is not indicative of overflow status.

4. Add (+ 1) to (+ 127)		01111111	+ 127	Accumulator
		00000001	+ 1	Operand data
	1	10000000	+ 128	Accumulator result

This time there is obviously an overflow condition because of the inherent restriction on the maximum positive number of 127. Notice that there was no carry.

From a study of these examples, is it possible to arrive at a valid statement which defines the conditions for overflow? They have shown that neither the presence of a carry or a change of sign are in themselves evidence so we must assume that the microprocessor arithmetic circuits must have an inbuilt overflow 'detector' which sets the V bit accordingly. Humans of course could easily deduce the conditions by simple reasoning as follows:

Adding two positive numbers must not exceed + 127 or overflow occurs.

Adding two negative numbers must not exceed −128 or overflow occurs.

Adding a positive to a negative can never cause overflow.

But this kind of reasoning is alien to computers — it is doubtful if they can reason at all anyway. And yet they can be trusted to the nth degree once the logic has been designed in accordance with the laws of Boolean algebra. Examination of the examples again reveals a rather strange but pertinent variation between the bit patterns of Example 4 (which did cause overflow) and the others (which did not).

> Overflow exists if the carry bit IN to sign position is different from the carry bit OUT of the sign position

Thus if the add process causes a '1' to be carried into the sign position and a '1' is carried out, there is no overflow; Example 2 illustrated this. Examine Example 4 again and confirm that a '1' was carried in to the sign position but a '0' was carried out; since they were different the V bit would be set. Computer logic can easily spot differences between bits by using an EXCLUSIVE-OR gate, which gives an output of '1' *only* if the two input bits are different. Thus, two '0's or two '1's would give a '0' output.

Single byte subtraction

If there were no facilities for subtraction as a separate instruction (such as SBC) it would still be possible to subtract numbers by using the 'add the complement' method.

Subtract (+ 3) from (+ 5)	+ 3	00000011
	two's complement is	11111101
	So if we add this complement it will be 'subtraction'	
	+ 5	00000101
	add complement of + 3	11111101
	1	00000010

Notice that again there is a carry out but no overflow status (the answer is correct). It is not expected that subtraction be carried out using this method but such knowledge can be useful on the odd occasion. There is, of course, in the 6502 the SBC instruction and as the name implies, it takes the carry into consideration. As mentioned earlier, it is necessary to *set* the carry (not clear it) before subtracting. This is because the computer implements SBC by using complementary addition, so it is essential to complement the carry bit with SEC beforehand.

Significance of the C and V bits

If an addition is carried out, the result is left in the Accumulator and the C and V bits are automatically set or reset as appropriate. But there the responsibility of the microprocessor ends. It doesn't stop or issue any warning if the result is invalid due to overflow — it sets the V bit, shrugs its shoulders and carries on with the next instruction. It would have been easy in the design stage to cause the computer to halt on overflow but this would be undesirable. It would rob the programmer of the ability to manoeuvre, to take advantage of the pathetic intellect of the computer. The programmer can decide whether or not to ignore the V bit because in certain circumstances the answer could be correct (from the programmer's viewpoint) even if the V bit is set. The C bit is often set or reset in instructions other than addition (ADC) or subtraction (SBC). The ability to take action or ignore the C and V bits is the key to the problem of 'multi-precision' arithmetic which overcomes the limitations imposed by an eight-bit result.

Multi-precision arithmetic

This is the technique of using *more than one* location or register to hold *one* item of data and organising the arithmetic instructions accordingly. Before describing the details of the technique we first consider a simple case to illustrate how the programmer will at times ignore the overflow status in order to expand the range of positive (or negative) numbers which can be held in a single byte result. If we refer to Example 4 in which the addition of + 1 to + 127 resulted in 'overflow', it is clearly allowable for a programmer to ignore this. If the numbers being dealt with are known in advance to be *all positive* there is little point in allowing space in a byte for the 'sign bit' and the result can be interpreted in *unsigned* binary. If this is so, the result 10000000 becomes 128 absolute. The maximum number which could be held is now 11111111 = 255 absolute. By ignoring the V bit and overriding the inherent two's complement nature of the internal arithmetic logic, it has been possible to double the range of absolute numbers provided that the ability to handle mixed sign is sacrificed. Suppose we proceed with this concept a stage further and use the C bit, not as an indication of a 'carry' but as a *ninth bit* of the Accumulator. This will allow us to double the range of unsigned numbers yet again. Thus, the maximum absolute number becomes

C   Accumulator
1   11111111 = 511 decimal

The carry bit, bearing in mind it represents (by virtue of its binary weighting) a value of $2^8 = 256$ decimal, must be added to the Accumulator contents (255 in total) to produce 511 decimal.

We now appear to have exhausted the expansion options available if the result is to be presented in *one go*. But why can't we use *two* locations in memory to hold the result? No reason at all why not — except that it is going to be a little more tricky to program because it will now be important to ensure that the results of each single byte are properly placed in the double byte locations. It is also important to be sure to know when to ignore the C and V bits and when to take them into consideration.

Adding single byte numbers into a double byte result

Program 19. Two numbers are in addresses 0370 and 0371. Add these and store the result in the pair of addresses 0372 (lower order byte of result) and 0373 (higher order byte). Assume numbers are in normal two's complement notation

LDA	#$00		A9	00	
STA	$0372	Clear Acc and result bytes	8D	72	03
STA	$0373		8D	73	03
LDA	$0372	Load lower order result	AD	72	03
CLC			18		
ADC	#$0370	Add first number	6D	70	03
STA	$0372	Store in low order result	8D	72	03
LDA	$0373	Load high order result	AD	73	03
ADC	#$00	Add Zero + carry bit	69	00	
STA	$0373	Store in high order result	8D	73	03
LDA	$0372	Load lower order result	AD	72	03
CLC			18		
ADC	#$0371	Add second number	6D	71	03
STA	$0372	Store in low order result	8D	72	03
LDA	$0373	Load high order result	AD	73	03
ADC	#$00	Add Zero + carry bit	69	00	
STA	$0373	Store in high order result	8D	73	03
BRK			00		

The first step was to clear the Acc and the two locations to hold the result. You may think not strictly necessary but it helps in understanding the logic flow.

The procedure for both numbers is identical (as can be seen by the dividing lines in the remarks column) so it is only necessary to understand the first. The lower order result byte is first loaded into the Acc and the first number added to it. No carry is added because the CLC previously cleared it. The Acc is stored in the lower order byte result which now contains an updated total. Next, the higher order result byte is loaded into the Acc and *zero* is added using immediate addressing, but this time, *with* the carry bit (if any). Although the double byte result occupies two memory locations we must visualise them as laid out end to end as follows:

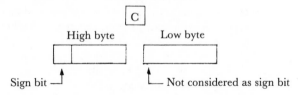

The sign of the double byte result is the msb of the high byte. The bit

usually taken to be the sign in the low byte is just treated as an ordinary magnitude bit. This allows 15 bits for magnitude with the C bit providing the linkage between the two bytes. The maximum positive number is now 01111111 11111111 which is $2^{15} - 1 = 32\ 767$ decimal and the maximum negative $-32\ 768$.

To understand the linkage via the C bit, study the following examples: Let the first number be 255 decimal, 11111111 in binary and the second be 128 decimal, 10000000. The pencil and paper working is

$$
\begin{array}{r}
11111111 \\
10000000 \\
\hline
1 \qquad 01111111 \quad \text{Result in low order byte.} \\
\hline
\end{array}
$$

Next, zero is added (plus carry) to the higher order byte giving 00000001.
The double byte result is therefore

$$00000001\ 01111111 = +383 \text{ decimal}$$

To see that it works we add yet another number

present total = 00000001 01111111 , add 129 decimal to low byte,

$$
\begin{array}{r}
10000001 \\
\hline
1 \qquad 00000000 \\
\hline
\end{array}
$$

add zero (plus carry) to the higher order byte giving 00000010.
The double byte result has now grown to

$$00000010\ 00000000 = 512 \text{ decimal}$$

The next program uses the same technique to add a list of numbers into a grand total.

Program 20. A block of single byte numbers are in addresses 0360 to 0369. Add these up and leave the double precision result in 0370 (low order byte) and 0371 (high order byte)

	LDX	#$00		A2	00	
	STX	$0370	Clear X and result bytes	8E	70	03
	STX	$0371		8E	71	03
BACK	LDA	$0370	Load low order byte result	AD	70	03
	CLC			18		
	ADC	#$0370, X	Add a number	7D	60	03
	STA	$0370	Store in low order byte result	8D	70	03
	LDA	$0371	Load high order byte result	AD	71	03
	ADC	#$00	Add Zero + carry bit	69	00	
	STA	$0371	Store in high order byte result	8D	71	03
	INX			E8		
	CPC	#$0A	All jobs done?	E0	0A	
	BNE	BACK	No	D0	E9	
	BRK		Yes	00		

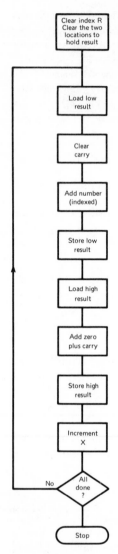

Clear index R
Clear the two
locations to
hold result

Load low
result

Clear
carry

Add number
(indexed)

Store low
result

Load high
result

Add zero
plus carry

Store high
result

Increment
X

All
done
?

No

Stop

Fig. 6.1. Flowchart of program 20

The flowchart shown in Fig. 6.1 will help in the understanding of Program 20.

Adding double-byte numbers

The procedure would be virtually identical to single byte additions.

88

The only difference is in the way higher order bytes are handled. Instead of adding 'zero plus carry' we must add 'higher order byte plus carry'.

Program 21. One number is held in a pair of addresses 0380 (low byte) and 0381 (high byte); the other number in 0382 and 0383. Add these up and store result in 0384 and 0385

LDA	00		A9	00	
STA	0384	Clear Acc and result bytes	8D	84	03
STA	0385		8D	85	03
LDA	0384	Load low byte result	AD	84	03
CLC			18		
ADC	0380	Add first number (low byte)	6D	80	03
STA	0384	Store in low byte result	8D	84	03
LDA	0385	Load high byte result	AD	85	03
ADC	0381	Add first number (high byte)	6D	81	03
STA	0385	Store in high byte result	8D	85	03
LDA	0384	Load low byte result	AD	84	03
CLC			18		
ADC	0384	Add second number (low byte)	6D	82	03
STA	0384	Store in low byte result	8D	84	03
LDA	0385	Load high byte result	AD	85	03
ADC	0383	Add second number (high byte)	6D	83	03
STA	0385	Store in high byte result	8D	85	03
BRK			00		

This appears a cumbersome method but apart from the first three lines (which are included for 'tidiness') there is no short cut. Before labouring through each line individually, it may help matters to picture the memory map:

0380	Low byte	1st number
0381	High byte	
0382	Low byte	2nd number
0383	High byte	
0384	Low byte	Result
0385	High byte	

It was stated that there were 'no short cuts' but this was not strictly true. Apart from the first three instructions, a further saving of a byte or so could have been obtained by *loading* the first number and adding the second. Indeed, if this program was literally intended to add only *two* numbers together it would certainly not require the first three instructions to clear the accumulator and the destination locations; i.e. it would not require *initialisation*. These remarks would also apply to Program 19. But these short cuts would prejudice the application of the program skeleton if it was later intended to add a series of numbers by means of indexed addressing. It is standard (and wise) procedure to initialise first before entering the indexing loop because the *process* is entirely ADC on all numbers in the list instead of a single STA for the first number and ADC for the rest — an awkward 'odd man out' situation.

The next program is the natural corollary because it takes the skeleton and fits it into an indexed loop. If we look back to Programs 19 and 20, it will be recognised that a similar relationship was involved.

Program 22. Five double byte numbers are stored in addresses 0380 to 0389. Add these up and store result in address 038A (low byte) and 038B (high byte)

	LDX	00		A2	00	
	STX	038A		8E	8A	03
	STX	038B		8E	8B	03
BACK	LDA	038A	Load low byte result	AD	8A	03
	CLC			18		
	ADC	0380, X	Add low byte (indexed)	7D	80	03
	STA	038A	Store low byte result	8D	8A	03
	INX			E8		
	ADC	0380, X	Add high byte (indexed)	7D	80	03
	STA	038B	Store high byte result	8D	8B	03
	INX			E8		
	CPX	0A	All done?	E0	0A	
	BNE	BACK		D0	EA	
	BRK			00		

Compare the program with Program 20 and note it is almost identical, the two differences being:

(a) Both ADCs act on money
(b) An extra INX is needed to bring out the higher byte of each number.

Double byte subtraction

It is unnecessary to treat the detailed mechanism with the aid of programs. The programs for adding numbers will also work for subtracting numbers provided:

(a) SEC is replaced by SEC (set carry).
(b) SBC is used in place of ADC.

BCD Addition and subtraction

The 6502 facility for performing arithmetic on BCD formatted numbers is to some extent unique. Some micros offer a kind of BCD arithmetic but demand some assistance from the programmer during each add or subtract instruction. On the 6502, it is a once and once only operation of setting the D bit at the head of the program. Any of the previous programs involving addition or subtraction will operate in BCD format provided that the initialisation lines include one extra instruction, SED (hex code F8). Once the D bit has been set, the micro will continue to treat all numbers as if they were in BCD format. If it is intended to revert to normal binary arithmetic in the same program, it would be necessary to clear the D bit with the instruction CLD (hex code 38).

One or two words of warning may be useful when using BCD:

(a) It is up to the programmer to ensure that numerical data presented to the ADC or SBC routines are indeed in BCD format. You will remember that four bit binary groupings 1010 to 1111 inclusive are illegal in BCD — these are in fact the nibbles which are represented in hex by the letters A to F inclusive.

(b) The operating system which runs the keyboard, screen and the BASIC interpreter almost always ensures that the D bit is cleared so it would be unnecessary in the previous programs to clear it at the head of every program. Normal binary would be assumed. However, if you are bold enough to bypass the operating system and run your machine code programs 'naked' you had better tell the machine what arithmetic you need because the power on conditions are indeterminate in the PSR.

Under what conditions would you use BCD? The answer is probably not very often. There are two main areas:

(a) Peripheral instrumentation normally outputs (or expects inputs to be) in BCD. If your programs are to handle these devices then your arithmetic must be compatible.

(b) Where *exact* money calculations are important. The high priests of a religion known as 'Chief Accountants' are not amused by the kind of rational rounding tolerated in physics or engineering. BCD calculations can be right to the penny — if enough places, or rather nibbles, are taken. 'Look after the pennies and the pounds will take care of themselves' is one of those archaic platitudes which are still taken literally in the Boardroom.

The power of shift, rotate and logic operations

Apart from multiplication and division by powers of two, the shift and rotate instructions are used to manipulate bits within a byte and, like the 'logical' instructions, are non-arithmetic in nature. Their use demands a certain amount of inspired trickery on the part of the programmer and many of the operations carried out appear mysterious. The actual mechanism of these operations have all been previously described although using them is not exactly straightforward. Instead of going step by step again over what each instruction does, it is more helpful to study some random program segments — they may come in useful to splice into your own programs.

Program 23. Single byte numbers of mixed sign are stored in addresses 0360 to 0369. Change them all to absolute values, i.e. if positive leave them alone, if negative change them to positive

	CLC			18		
	LDX	#$00		A2	00	
BACK	LDA	0360, A	Load a number (indexed)	BD	60	03
	BPL	SKIP	Skip the next three if positive	10	07	
	EOR	#$FF	Change all the bits (one's compl.)	49	FF	
	ADC	#$01	Add one to form two's compl.	69	01	
	STA	$0360, X	Replace in positive form	9D	60	03
SKIP	INX			E8		
	CPX	#$0A	All done?	E0	0A	
	BNE	BACK	No	D0	EF	
	BRK		Yes	00		

To change the sign of a number you convert it to the two's complement, by first *changing* all the bits. To change a bit, EXCLUSIVE-OR it with a '1'. So to change all the bits, EXCLUSIVE-OR it with FF. After this, one is added (by ADC immediate 01) and the now positive number is restored in its original home.

Coded records

By storing records in coded form, a surprising amount of information can be squeezed into a single byte. The actual code used is not important and, provided that it is used consistently, can be home-made. Apart from the economy in memory requirements, coded information obviously carries certain advantages in the area of security.

To illustrate the method and to provide a guinea-pig for experimenting with logic tricks examine the following simple code.

92

Sample code for computer dating

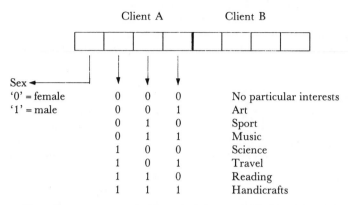

| Client A | Client B |

| | | | | | | | |

Sex ◄
'0' = female   0   0   0   No particular interests
'1' = male   0   0   1   Art
               0   1   0   Sport
               0   1   1   Music
               1   0   0   Science
               1   0   1   Travel
               1   1   0   Reading
               1   1   1   Handicrafts

Two clients are squeezed into each byte and distinguished by the 'A' nibble (left byte) and the 'B' nibble (right byte). The coding is shown for client A although the relative bit positions apply also to client B.

Examples: If client A was coded F hex, he would be interested in handicrafts.
If client A was coded 3 hex, she would be interested in music.
If the contents of a complete byte was coded 4A, client A would be a female scientist and client B a male sportsman.

It should be emphasised that the code is primitive and does not contain the sophistication expected in a real situation. A computer dating service would normally include personal characteristics of a more intimate nature but this is a family book and it would be indelicate to include them. It does however serve the purpose of showing how even four bits can hide quite a lot of information. It is left to the imagination to visualise the enormous possibilities if say, two complete bytes were allotted to each client — 65 536 distinct categories! If stored in 'plain language' characters in BASIC, two bytes would only hold *two characters*. Of course, the actual printing out of the matched data would have to be human oriented and delivered in normal English but the point is — the actual storage of large amounts of data can be achieved most economically if binary coded.

Having stored this data, how can it be manipulated? Using two clients for each byte has of course introduced complications but this is all to the good, because it provides an excellent example in the use of the shift or rotate instructions in 'unpacking' data. Before offering a complete program which searches for a match it would help to examine each separate problem associated with the task.

1. If a match is found, how is the particular client identified?

   The hex address itself can be the client's identification code with a flag bit somewhere to identify which particular nibble within that address. Thus, a client whose identification code was 063F (B) would indeed be stored in the *right hand nibble* of hex address 063F.

2. How can the two halves be separated once in the Accumulator?

   There are several ways, but the easiest would be to PSH a copy in the stack first then AND mask the 'B' nibble to all zeros. This leaves the 'A' nibble on its own. To handle the 'B' nibble, the original can be retrieved from the stack with PLA and shifted four places left. This will kick out the 'A' nibble and leave the 'B' nibble in the processing position at the left:

```
PSH                      Save on stack
AND  #$FO                Erase the 'B' nibble
(process client A)
PLA                      Retrieve from stack
ASL A
ASL A                    Kick out the 'A' nibble
ASL A                    and bring 'B' nibble to left.
ASL A
(process client B)
```

3. Assuming the nibble is in the left position, how is sex determined?

   The sex bit is in the sign position so BPL or BMI can be the test branch.

4. What is the 'process'?

   This depends on you but the most probable requirement would be to test if the client satisfied a certain match. This is easily done by AND masking followed by a BNE or BEQ, whichever is the more convenient.

   The next program is useful for testing out the ideas described. The total of clients stored is low but is quite sufficient for test purposes.

Program 24. Twenty clients are stored in addresses 0370 to 0379 in the code form described previously. How many of them are ladies interested in science? Answer in address 037A (see Fig. 6.2)

	LDX	#$00	Clear index	A2 00
	STX	037A	Clear address to hold total	8E 7A 03
BACK	LDA	0360, X	Load two clients, indexed	BD 70 03
	PHA		Save copy on stack	48
	AND	#$F0	Erase client B	29 F0
	BMI	SKIP	Reject if male	30 09

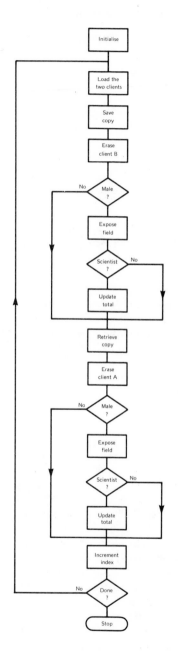

Fig. 6.2. Flowchart for program 24

95

	AND	#$70	Erase all bits except 'interest' field	29	70	
	SEC			38		
	SBC	#$40	(01000000) is female scientist	E9	40	
	BNE	SKIP	Reject (no match)	D0	03	
	INC	0370	Add one to total	EE	70	03
SKIP	PLA		Retrieve copy from stack	68		
	ASL	A		0A		
	ASL	A	Bring client B to left	0A		
	ASL	A		0A		
	ASL	A		0A		
	BMI	SKIP1	Reject if male	30	09	
	AND	#$70	Erase all bits except 'interest' field	29	70	
	SEC			38		
	SBC	#$40	(01000000) is female scientist	E9	40	
	BNE	SKIP1	Reject (no match)	D0	03	
	INC	0730	Add one to total	EE	70	03
SKIP1	INX			E8		
	CPX	#$0A	All jobs done?	E0	0A	
	BNE	BACK	No	D0	DA	
	BRK			00		

It should be emphasised that the program is intended only to illustrate the use of logical and shift instructions with little attention being paid to the coding efficiency. In fact it is apparent from the flowchart that a sizeable chunk of code is repeated twice and could have been reduced by using an inner loop.

ASCII code manipulations

A keyboard character, in the majority of computers, is stored in the form of a seven-bit code known as ASCII which stands for 'American Standard Code for Information Interchange'. It is mercifully pronounced as 'Askey'. There is room in the code for 128 different characters ($2^7 = 128$) and most of them are used. The total character set can be divided into upper case letters A — Z, lower case letters a — z, the digits 0 — 9, various punctuation symbols including the dollar sign (which of course emphasises the American origin) and the ubiquitous hash mark # . Appendix 2 includes a restricted set of the most used ASCII characters with their hex and decimal equivalents. The full code includes various 'control' characters and odds and ends which tend to obscure the most commonly used letters and figures. It is useful to be aware of the basic structure of the code in order to manipulate the bits. The following is the broad plan which holds for letters and figures:

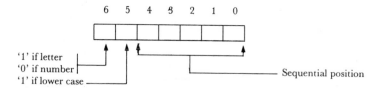

| | | 6 | 5 | 4 | 3 | 2 | 1 | 0 |

'1' if letter
'0' if number
'1' if lower case

Sequential position

The five least significant bits are used for alphabetical sequence purposes. Thus the upper case 'E' which is the fifth character would have the ASCII code 1000101 (hex 45) or decimal 69. Lower case 'e' would be 1100101 (hex 65) or decimal 101. Numbers are also found by the code sequence except that *bit 4 is always a '1'*. Thus, '9' is coded 0111001 (hex 39) or decimal 57. Remember that numbers on a typewriter are always lower case.

Suppose we are entering numbers, 'numerical digits' is the posh term, it is clear that the only bits of the code which are strictly numerical are the four least significant bits, the remaining bits are so much garbage *if we know* that the characters expected are indeed numbers. So the first job in a keyboard read segment would be to strip off the unwanted bits using an AND mask technique.

Before attempting to illustrate masking it would be advisable to deal with the missing eight bit. Since the ASCII code is a seven-bit code, what do they do with the eighth bit at the msb end? There is no hard and fast rule in microcomputers. Traditionally, the eight bit was used to check *parity* but this 'waste' of a bit is seldom found except perhaps in minicomputers or mainframes. It is now often used for the 'reverse print' mode. Thus, if the eighth bit is a '0', the mode is normal; if however the eighth bit is '1' it signifies reverse print (black on white instead of white on black or some alternative colour scheme). Study of the User's Manual of your micro will establish the point.

There are only two areas within the computer where the ASCII code would normally be used, the keyboard input, the screen memory and the area of RAM where character strings are stored.

Program 25. Numbers in ASCII code format are stored in addresses 0360 to 0369. Convert them to BCD format

	LDX	00	Clear index	A2	00	
BACK	LDA	0360, X	Load ASCII (indexed)	BD	60	03
	AND	0F	Erase the four left hand bits	29	0F	
	STA	0360, X	Replace	9D	60	03
	INX			E8		
	CPX	0A	All done?	E0	0A	
	BNE	BACK	No	D0	F3	
	BRK		Yes	00		

The previous program was an easy example because of the prior knowledge. The problem of separating numerics from punctuation and letters or in general, a complete analysis of ASCII characters involves examination of the three higher order bits. Shift instructions are useful for moving bit patterns into the sign position in order to test (by means of BPL or BMI) if a particular bit is set. The BIT test is useful in this area because of the power it possesses of pin-pointing bits 6 and 7 *whilst still in memory*. Since shifts can also be carried out whilst still in memory it is quite possible to gain a good deal of information without even troubling the Accumulator.

For example, suppose in location 0360 is an ASCII pattern. If we ASL one place, bits 5 and 6 of the ASCII become bits 6 and 7, both of which can be tested by BVC and BMI.

Thus   ASL 0360
        BIT 0360

After this, we know that if the original ASCII bit 6 was a '1', the N bit in the PSR would be set and if bit 5 was a '1', the V bit would be set.

Using the EOR and ORA

Although these two are 'logical' they find their greatest use in the field of Input/Output manipulation and will be treated later under that heading.

The program examples in this chapter should provide at least food for thought and you would be well advised to enter all of them and any dummy data they demand. Most of the data has been assumed to lie in addresses 0360 onwards but this is only because the writer tried them out on a CBM microcomputer and this area is convenient for this machine. It is a simple matter to rearrange the operand addresses if the data must lie elsewhere. All programs have ended with BRK but if RTS is substituted they could be used as subroutines provided pre-preparation techniques were arranged prior to calling.

Summary

- Before starting an Adding sequence, reset the carry bit with CLC.
- Before starting a Subtract sequence, set the carry with SEC.
- The C bit and the V bit, although updated by the computer automatically, are there only for the programmer's information and can be ignored.

- When adding single byte numbers into a double byte result the carry is first cleared and the lower byte is added and returned to the lower byte result. Next zero plus carry is added to the higher byte result.

- To add double byte numbers into a double byte result, the procedure is similar to the above but instead of adding zero plus carry, the higher order byte plus carry is used.

- BCD arithmetic is easy on the 6502. Just remember to set the D bit first with SED. Also remember to clear it again with CLD if reversion to normal two's complement arithmetic is to follow.

- To obtain the two's complement, use EOR FF then add 1.

- A home made binary code can be a very economical dodge to store personnel or indeed any kind of records.

- The ASCII code (pronounced Askey) is the popular code for storing keyboard characters.

- The full ASCII uses seven bits and allows 128 different characters including various control codes. An abbreviated form of the ASCII is given in Appendix 2.

- The eighth bit is often used to signify 'reverse character' display.

7

Input/output manipulations

What is peripheral?

Anything which is used by, but is not an integral part of, a computer is deserving of the name *peripheral*. Obvious peripherals are, of course, floppy disks, cassette recorders and printers but the two things we do not normally (but should) treat as peripherals are the keyboard and the video screen. There are many more exotic devices which can now be hooked on to the computer including light pens, 'writing tablets', voice recorders, joysticks — the list is growing every month. It is all part of an anthropomorphic desire to invest computer systems with 'human' senses, although some of them are little short of gimmicks. Voice operated systems have always intrigued us and science fiction writers worth their salt must include an ORAC or a ZEN in the scenario. Perhaps the technique will improve but at present, the primitive Dalek type accents of the first generation systems seem preferable to the latest craze towards re-creating the old 'Oxford' accent.

Another important range of peripherals are the ON/OFF control lines which activate mechanical systems and move robot arms or wash clothes etc. This is an interesting area for the model enthusiast who is also a computer type.

Interface problems

The kindest thing you can say about most peripherals is that they exhibit individualism. In short, they are undisciplined, lazy, greedy and loudmouthed. The thousands of circuits *within* the computer boundary behave like well drilled soldiers obeying instantaneously the commands of the microprocessor master clock. Everything is synchronised to the clock and order reigns throughout. Peripherals tend to sneer at the clock and go their own way. Internal circuits operate at high speed using a time scale in the order of microseconds. Peripherals are sluggish, their full-out speed seldom breaking the millisecond barrier. The power consumption of the internal computing circuits is modest. A typical hairy chested peripheral can eat up more power than the entire computing system. They have a lust for current and voltage. The internal computing system operates in an acoustical vacuum. Peripherals either clack or they hum or they clatter like an ageing lawnmower. A typical line printer, when feeling particularly cheerful, can drown Concorde. As might be expected, the difference in temperament between peripheral and computer causes problems.

The problems come under the general heading of *interfacing*. There are two of them:

(a) Hardware interfacing: electronic circuitry is required to compensate for the different voltage and current requirements. These problems are outside the scope of this book.

(b) Software interfacing: program segments are required to compensate for the different timing requirements.

Interface chips

The manufacturers of microprocessors always offer support chips forming a 'family', each member of which is electrically and software compatible with the rest. Thus the general family title of our system is the 650X, the X number determining the particular member. Thus, the microprocessor itself is the 6502 and the 6520 is an input output chip called by the grandiose title of 'Peripheral Interface Adaptor' (known affectionately in the trade as a PIA). There is an even bigger and better input/output chip, the 6522 which is more versatile than the PIA and is correspondingly named the 'Versatile Interface Adaptor' (VIA for short).

Both the PIA and the VIA have quite complex interiors; in fact as far as number of pins are concerned they are equal in status to the microprocessor itself — 40 pins. The detailed treatment of these two chips would, to do them both justice, justify a separate book. The PIA is the simpler of the two and will be explained first.

The PIA (6520)

This chip consists of two virtually identical halves and to avoid much repetition only the 'A' side will be treated (the 'B' side differences are not serious).

Fig. 7.1 shows the programmer's view of the PIA (A side only) and note that it is connected to the address bus and the data bus of the microprocessor. This brands it immediately as a *memory mapped*

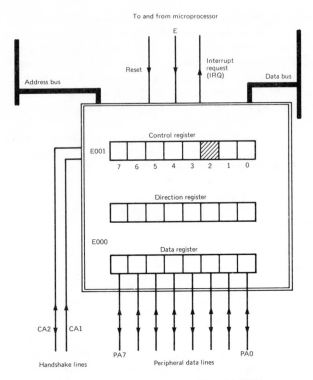

To and from microprocessor

E

Reset

Interrupt
request
(IRQ)

Address bus

Data bus

Control register

E001

7 6 5 4 3 2 1 0

Direction register

E000

Data register

CA2 CA1

PA7

PA0

Handshake lines

Peripheral data lines

Fig. 7.1. Peripheral interface adaptor (A side only) 6520

input/output chip; the registers within the chip are allocated unique
addresses and behave like any other memory locations. The particular
addresses allocated are in the first instance quite arbitrary but in the
case of a home computer system they have been decided once and for
all by the system designer. If you are proficient with a soldering iron
and would like to hook the PIA onto a different address area, you are
free in principle to do so but do make sure you know what you are
doing. Most of the address space has probably been allocated anyway
although if you decide to wire in another PIA (or even another dozen!)
you may find a few left.

What are the addresses?

This depends on your particular system so we shall *assume* the addresses
are as shown on Fig. 7.1.

There are three programmable registers but, for some strange reason, the original designers were stingy enough to restrict the number of addresses to two. One register has its own address, the other two have to *share* one address. Before attempting to define these registers study Fig. 7.1 closely and notice the double direction arrows on the eight *peripheral data lines*. These lines can be individually programmed to be either *inputs* from a peripheral or *outputs* to a peripheral. Taking any line at random, it is clear that it cannot at the *same time* be both an input and an output so we can understand why there is one special register used to define the direction of each.

First some definitions:

The eight data lines (PA0 to PA7)

These deliver or accept TTL voltage levels or, to phrase this a little less pompously, they can be switched ON or OFF. They are the main data paths between the peripheral/s and the microprocessor.

The data register (located at our assumed address E000)

This is a buffer or 'holding' register for the data lines.

The direction register (located at our assumed address E000)

By setting bit patterns in this register, the programmer can set the directivity of the data lines in accordance with the following convention:

A '1' in the direction register makes the corresponding data line an *output*.

A '0' in the direction register makes the corresponding data line an *input*.

Examples: With FF in the direction register, all data lines behave as *outputs*.

With F8 in the direction register, data lines PA3 to PA7 behave as outputs and data lines PA0 to PA2 behave as inputs.

The control register (Located at our assumed address E001)

With the sole exception of bit 2 (shown shaded in Fig. 7.1) this register is dedicated to the behaviour of the two handshake lines CA1 and CA2.

It must be admitted that this register is a bit of a swine to understand and the gory details will be left for later treatment. We must however be familiar with the use of bit 2 since it is vital to the behaviour of the Direction Register.

In fact it is bit 2 which resolves the problem of the 'shared address'. You will note again from Fig. 7.1 that the Direction and Data registers share the same address 8000 as how does the PIA know which is meant? The rule is simple:

If bit 2 is '0', the address E000 is the Direction Register.
If bit 2 is '1', the address E000 is the Data Register.

Under reset conditions, all the registers in the PIA have their bits cleared to '0's so initially, bit 2 is '0' and consequently the Address E000 must refer to the Direction Register. After the desired bit pattern is set in this register, the contents of the Control Register can be changed to allow future references to E000 to belong exclusively to the Data Register. If the handshake lines are not being used (and they don't always have to be) the remaining bits of the Control Register can remain at zero. It will be appreciated that the directivity of the data lines are unlikely to require changing within the same program or system so setting the Direction Register is usually a one-off job during the program initialisation. It would be well to study a few simple examples of initialisation in order to sort out all this conglomeration.

Example: Initialise the PIA to cause all the data lines to behave as outputs. Do not assume that reset action has occurred.

```
LDA   #$00    Clear Acc
STA   $E001   Clear Control register
LDA   #$FF
STA   $E000   Put all '1's in Direction Register
LDA   #$04
STA   $E001   Set bit 2 to '1' in Control Register
```

Note the hex number 04 in the Control register (00000100) which sets bit 2. Although the initialisation example set the required *directivity* of the output lines it is well to note that the actual logic voltages on each output are not yet established. All we have told the PIA up to now is that the eight data lines are to *behave* as outputs. To set the patterns of '1's and '0's the lines must adopt, will require the corresponding bit pattern to be set into the Data Register. In future, to avoid repetition, we shall assume that reset conditions have been prior established so that there is no need for the Control Register to be cleared in the first instance.

Example: Initialise the PIA for PA0 and PA3 to be inputs and the remainder outputs.

```
LDA   #$F6
STA   E000    Put 11110110 in Direction Register
LDA   #$04    Set bit '2' to 1 in Control Register
STA   8001
```

Data lines programmed to behave as *inputs* will not accept patterns placed in the Data Register *from* the microprocessor. Thus, if all the lines are inputs and we store the bit pattern at, say, FF in the Data Register the dta lines will ignore it. This is understandable when you think about it — if a line is supposed to be an input, then the only legitimate signal must come from outside.

The handshake lines

The PIA is equipped with two special lines CA1 and CA2 which are primarily used to keep peripherals and computer in step with each other. CA1 can only be used as an input but CA2 can be programmed to behave either as an input or an output, depending on the state of a certain bit in the Control Register. In fact, the behaviour of the handshake lines is intimately linked with the pattern set in the Control Register. These details will be left until we discuss the subject of *interrupts*.

Programmable test panel

It is advisable to practise on simple examples before attempting ambitious projects. Writing bug-proof software to control peripherals can be a lengthy task and can lead to much gnashing of teeth before they begin to behave. It is a good plan to construct a test panel which can be used for gaining confidence before risking your talents on real equipment. The primary requirements of such a panel are to *display* the states of the data lines and to provide simulated *inputs*. Fig. 7.2 is a circuit diagram of such a panel which provides crude but quite effective simulation of peripheral behaviour. Before detailed descriptions are given, a word of warning is advisable. Unless you have some experience in the construction of electronic equipment (particularly

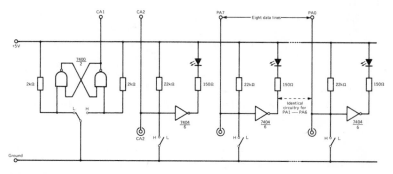

Fig. 7.2

105

digital) it is better to enlist the aid of someone who has! Home computers are not cheap and connecting badly constructed gadgets could turn out to be an expensive exercise. The drawing is shown in adequate detail to guide those with prior experience. The appearance and mechanical details of the front panel are left to your own imagination and artistic sense. The power supply can be obtained from either:

1. Stealing from the computer's 5 V supply (if your knowledgeable friend thinks there are enough milliamps available).
2. Constructing a mains 5 V supply. (Particular care required here!)
3. Using dry batteries. Unfortunately, 5 V is an awkward value for batteries but 4.5 V would be quite suitable. In fact dry batteries are the safest method of all.

Panel facilities

(1) Simple switches provide simulated inputs to the PIA data lines. One special switched input is used to feed CA1 because of the more demanding requirements.
(2) Light emitting diodes (LEDs) are used to indicate the logic state of the outputs. They light up when an output is in the HIGH state (logic 1).
(3) Sockets are provided which are direct connections to the data and handshake lines. These can be used to drive (or be driven by) external devices. To safeguard against unwanted voltage pulses feeding back into the PIA, it is essential that the sockets 'see' a TTL device as the first load. This device can be an inverting or non-inverting buffer.

Before example programs and hook-ups are given, there are a few quirks to be aware of with regard to the switch positions and the meanings to be attached to the LED displays (see Fig. 7.3).

When a line is to be used as an *output* the appropriate switch must be left in the 'H' position (switched OFF) otherwise the line is rigidly grounded and the PIA is unable to pull it to the HIGH state. The PIA outputs are in the 'floating high' state until the Direction Register has been initialised so all the LEDs will be in the ON state when the panel is connected but programs have not been run. LEDs will go to the OFF state only when the Data Register has been loaded with '0's.

The panel should be connected via a suitable multiway plug/socket to the User Port but again, a warning that such connections should only be made after consulting the hardware section of your User's

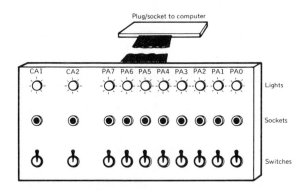

Fig. 7.3

Manual. The following programs will assume that the panel or some equivalent is indeed connected to the computer User Port. It also assumes of course that the User Port is driven by a PIA chip, either a 6520 or a 6820. It is fortunate that another very popular chip found in microprocessor controlled computers is very similar to the PIA; it is in fact called a VIA meaning 'Versatile Interface Adaptor'. This chip may be thought of as our PIA plus much more. The full facilities of a VIA include internal counters and hardware shift registers, all of which can be under program control. Whether the User Port is a PIA or a VIA, the panel connections will be broadly the same, the main difference (apart from the extras) is that a VIA has a completely separate address for the Direction Register and the pin we have called CA1 my be CB1 instead.

Program 26. Make the data lines all outputs with the four right hand lights ON and the four left hand lamps OFF

LDA	# $00	Clear Acc and Control Register	A9	00
STA	E001		8D	01 E0
LDA	#,$FF	Set all '1's in Direction Register	A9	FF
STA	E000		8D	00 E0
LDA	#,$04	Set bit 2 in Control Register	A9	04
STA	E000		8D	00 E0
LDA	#,$0F	4 R.H. lamps ON	A9	0F
STA	E000		8D	00 E0
BRK			00	

This program invites the obvious criticism — what a tedious job just to switch four lights on! We must remember however that initialising the PIA is a 'one off' job and in a complex program the above lines would represent a small part of the total number of lines. We should also

107

understand that we can't have the best of both worlds. If we want the luxury and versatility of a 100% programmable device then we must expect a certain amount of tedium in order for it to behave in the particular manner required for one purpose. Don't forget when trying out the program to leave all the input switches OFF (in the H position). Remember also that a lamp ON in any position will cause the corresponding socket outlet to assume the logic HIGH position (logic 1). If you have a logic probe or similar detector, you should confirm these statements.

Program 27. Use the four left-hand data input switches to control the four right hand lamps

	CLV			B8	
	LDA	#$00	Clear Acc and X	A9	00
	TAX			AA	
	STA	$E001	Clear Control Register	8D 01	E0
	LDA	#$0F	Set Direction Register	A9	0F
	STA	E000		8D 00	E0
	LDA	#$04	Set bit 2 in Control Register	A9	04
	STA	$E001		8D 01	E0
	STX	$E000	Clear Data Register	8E 00	E0
BACK	LDA	$E000	Load switch pattern into Acc	AD 00	E0
	LSR	A	Shift left nibble along to	4A	
	LSR	A	right nibble	4A	
	LSR	A		4A	
	LSR	A		4A	
	STA	$E000	Set lamp pattern	8D 00	E0
	BVC	BACK	Close switch sensing loop	50	F4

The program is closed loop, continuously sensing the current positions of the switches. There is no unconditional BRANCH instruction in the 6502 so a back-door method using the BVC test is used. The branch will always be taken because the V bit is initially cleared and none of the instructions subsequently used will affect the V bit.

The switches provide input for PA4 to PA7 and the four LSR lines move the pattern into the PA0 to PA3 position ready for displaying the lamps. There is no ways of breaking out of this program once it has been started so it would be advisable to add a few more lines enabling the operator to switch an exit. However, this would entail the use of one of the handshake lines and would introduce unecessary complication at this stage.

108

Program 28. Cause the eight lamps to flash on and off continuously. The flashes to be at reasonable rate for normal vision

	CLV			B8		
	LDA	#$00	Clear Control Register	A9	00	
	STA	$E001		8D	01	E0
	LDA	#$FF	Set data lines all outputs	A9	FF	
	STA	$E000		8D	00	E0
	LDA	#$04	Set bit 2 in Control Register	A9	04	
	STA	$E001		8D	01	E0
	LDA	#$00	Switch lamps OFF	A9	00	
	STA	$E000		00	E0	
BACK	LDA	$70	Place a 'delay' number in Acc prior to using subroutine	A9	70	
	JSR	DELAY	(Program 15)	20	??	??
	LDA	$E000	Change over the lamp states by	AD	00	E0
	LDA	#$FF	exclusive-or with all the '1's	49	FF	
	STA	$E000		8D	00	E0
	BVC	BACK		50	F1	

If lights are flashed at computer speed, the display would just be a blurr. Use is made of an earlier program which was written as a subroutine with the delay time determined by the number left in the Acc prior to calling (refer to Program 15). Experiment with numbers other than 70 hex to vary the rate of flashing.

The address code where the subroutine lodges will depend on your own memory map so the operand in the machine code version has been left undetermined. If the assembler you have provides for symbolic operands then the word 'DELAY' would be acceptable provided of course that you used this in the label field of the subroutine.

The handshake lines

CA1 and CA2 should be thought of as data *control* lines rather than data lines. Most commonly used peripherals act too slowly for the computer so some kind of dialogue must be programmed between the two. Thus the computer may ask the peripheral 'Are you ready to receive data?' The peripheral may respond either with 'Yes' or 'No'. The conversations are naturally less refined than this but the meaning is the same.

Re-affirming an earlier statement:

CA1 can only be used as an *input*.
CA2 can be used as an *input* or an *output*

The CA1 input is a little unusual in behaviour and is described as an *edge-triggering* input. This means that something happens only if the input signal *changes* from one level to another. A logic *high* by itself will do nothing, neither will a logic *low*. Things only start to happen when the signal rises from low to high or (depending on a certain bit in the control register) falls form high to low.

Before describing the details of programming, study Fig. 7.4 which shows a method of connecting an analogue-to-digital converter (A/D converter) to the PIA. This is a device that accepts an analogue voltage

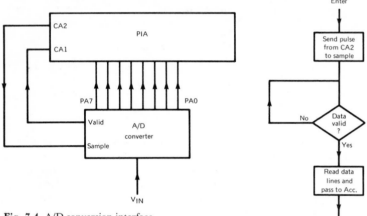

Fig. 7.4. A/D conversion interface

Fig. 7.5. 'Wait till ready' loop

at its input and then laboriously converts this to a set of binary bits which represent the value of the analogue voltage. Thus the input voltage may be anything within the range say, zero volts to 2.55 V. The corresponding binary output would be 00000000 to 11111111 which in pure unsigned binary would represent zero to 255 decimal. To achieve this conversion takes time — perhaps as long as a millisecond! Now a millisecond to us seems a negligible time but to a computer it is a couple of weeks. The A/D converter is therefore equipped with two handshake lines in addition to the eight data outputs. On receipt of a logic pulse from CA2 to the SAMPLE input, the A/D conversion process commences. When the binary data on the output lines is considered (by the A/D converter) to be a valid representation of V_{IN} it changes the state of the VALID output line. The 'conversation' would read something like this, 'Please start digitising' which eventually brings the reply 'I have done this so you can read in my data'. Fig. 7.5 illustrates in flow chart form the conversation. In a real situation, the analogue voltage V_{IN} would

110

probably be continually changing so it would be necessary to re-sample the data at regular intervals. The flowchart shown would then represent only a part of the complete 'read data' routine.

Programming CA1 and CA2

The behaviour of these lines is determined by the bit pattern placed in the control register during the initialisation routine, normally somewhere near the head of the program. The following description is based on Fig. 7.6 which defines the function of each bit in the Control Register. In spite of the forbidding appearance it is not too bad in practice to handle the register. Nevertheless, some additional comments may help in gaining confidence.

Note first that three bits 7, 1, 0 are concerned with the behaviour of the CA1 line. Four bits 6, 5, 4, 3 are concerned with CA2 line. The remaining bit 2 is the odd man out and has nothing to do with the handshake lines; it is our old 'friend' which is always set to '1' after the direction register has been tidied up.

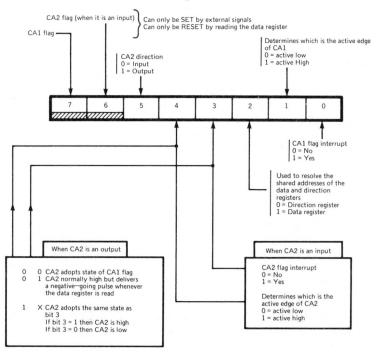

Fig. 7.6. Details of control register in PIA

CA1 Flag bit (bit 7)

This bit can *not* be directly programmed. It can only be set to 1 by the arrival of an external signal (of the correct polarity) on the CA1 line. Once the flag is set, it cannot be reset directly! It is reset automatically the next time the data register is *read*. 'Reading' the data register means performing an LDA, an LDX or an LDY.

CA2 Flag bit (bit 6)

When CA2 is programmed to behave as an input, bit 6 acts as the flag with the same properties as described under CA1.

CA2 Direction (bit 5)

To cause CA2 to behave as an input, this bit must be reset to 0. If this is changed to 1, CA2 becomes an output.

Bits 4 and 3

A complication arises here because the properties of these two bits are completely different, depending on whether CA2 is an input or an output. Assume first that CA2 is an *input*:

Bit 4 allows you to decide which *edge* of the CA2 input will set CA2 flag. If bit 4 is 0 then only when CA2 input *falls* from HIGH to LOW will the flag be set. If bit 4 is 1, a *rise* from LOW to HIGH is required.

Bit 3 determines whether INTERRUPT action is required when the CA2 flag is set. If bit 3 is 0, there is no interrupt action. If bit 3 is 1, an interrupt 'request' is sent from the PIA to the microprocessor.

The subject of interrupt will not be discussed in detail until later.
Assume that CA2 is an *output*:

CA2 flag (bit 6) ceases to have any relevance and the behaviour of CA2 depends on the particular permutation of bits 4 and 3 as shown in the kind of *truth table* shown at bottom left of Fig. 7.6 so each of these three permutations should be treated separately:

Bit 4 and 3 both 0

CA2 may be considered 'connected' to CA1 flag bit. Thus as soon as a signal arrives on CA1 which sets the flag bit, CA2 line immediately goes to the high state. It remains high until the flag bit is reset.

Bit 4 = 0 and bit 3 = 1

This permutation is used when a peripheral requires a 'negative-going' pulse, a typical example being the well known (to electronic types) 555 timer. CA2 will normally reset in the high state but whenever the data register is 'read' (by an LDA, LDX or an LDY) CA2 jumps low for a brief instant and then automatically returns back to the high state. To be more specific, the return occurs on the next falling edge of the 'E' line. This line is coincident with phase two of the microprocessor clock (refer back to Fig. 7.1).

Bit 4 = 1

If this bit is held at 1, CA2 is said to be in the 'manual' mode although it is not exactly a wise choice of label. In point of fact, CA2 will now adopt the state of bit 3. Changing bit 3 will cause the corresponding change in CA2 output state.

Bits 1 and 0

These belong to the CA1 line, having the same significance as bits 4 and 3 had on CA2 when an input.

Bit 1 determines which is the effective edge of CA1. Thus if bit 1 is 0 then a change of CA1 from high to low will set CA1 flag but if it is 1, only a change from low to high will be effective.

Bit 0 is the interrupt bit. If it is 0, then no interrupt occurs when the CA1 flag is set. If it is 1, then an interrupt request is sent immediately the CA1 flag is set.

This concludes the rather grim details of the PIA 'A' side. The 'B' side (if it is available for user port handling) is virtually identical to the 'A' side except for one or two variations. Thus on the 'B' side, the flags are automatically reset when the data register is 'written' into (after a STA, STX or STY). Before attempting actual programs using the handshake lines it is advisable to practise on the bit patterns required in the control register for various system requirements. In the examples which follow, the rule will be to place '0's in any bits which are either not used or conversely, which are not programmable. You will remember that bits 6 and 7 are not directly programmable so these will have '0's in them as far as our initialisation examples are concerned.

Example 1.   Assume CA1 is to be an active high input but not to cause interrupt. CA2 is to be an active low input and to cause interrupt.

(The term 'active low' means a change from high to low sets flat while 'active high' means from low to high.)

The correct pattern required in the control register is 00001110 (hex 0E). Thus after the data direction register has been initialised, the next lines would be:

    LDA   #$0E
    STA $E001

(In these examples, we shall stick with our assumption that the control register is located at address E001.)

Example 2.   Assume CA1 is to be active low input with no interrupt and CA2 the same.

The correct pattern required in the control register is 00000100 (04 hex). It is interesting that this example appears to be the default pattern because you may remember that in our examples, prior to discussing the handshake lines, we put 04 hex in the control register.

Example 3.   CA1 to be an active high input without interrupt. CA2 to be an output with the state to be initially low but subsequently to be determined by bit 3.

The correct pattern required in the control register is 00110110 (hex 36).

Example 4.   CA1 to be active low input causing interrupt. CA2 to be an output which is a negative going pulse coincident with a read of the data register.

The correct pattern required in the control register is 00101101 (hex 2D).

Example 5.   CA1 to be active high and cause interrupt. CA2 to be an output which copies the state of the CA1 flag bit.

The correct pattern required in the control register is 00100111 (hex 27).

Once the mechanics of the control register have been mastered the next logical step is to apply the technique to real situations. In the home computer field it may often be found that the user port facilities are less than adequate. Eight data lines and two handshake lines may often appear to restrict applications. It may happen that a certain project requires say, sixteen data lines and more handshakes. These situations call for ingenuity in the use of the available system which in turn

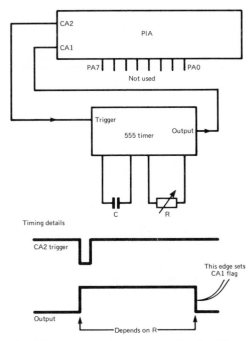

Fig. 7.7. Conversion of resistor control knob to binary

demands some expertise in the use of additional integrated circuits, decoders, multiplexers etc. With a little thought it is often possible to devise a peripheral system which uses 'less wires'.

As an example of user port economics, study Fig. 7.7 which shows how an external variable resistor (imagine this to be a joystick knob) can be persuaded to convert itself into a binary number by using only the two handshake lines, leaving the data lines free for other purposes. The solution to any computerised system naturally requires software as well as hardware, which is why interfacing engineers must be reasonably proficient in both fields. For example, it would be no good suggesting the hardware shown in Fig. 7.7 unless the designer had a reasonable idea of the kind of software back up needed to complete the system. Before treating the software, it is necessary to understand (roughly) the behaviour of the 555 timer chip. Consider it as a black box with one input and one output terminal which has the following property:

1. The output normally rests in the low state, the input in the high state.

2. If the input is momentarily driven low by a short duration pulse, the output goes high and *remains so* for a time depending on the value of an external capacitor (normally fixed) and a resistor (normally a variable).

Summarising, one negative-going pulse applied to the input causes a change of state at the output which eventually returns back to the initial resting state. The time interval which elapses before the return depends on both the C and R value of the external components. The timing details are shown in Fig. 7.7. A suitable software subroutine which handles the system is now tackled.

Program 29. Subroutine to place a value in the X register proportional to the current value of the variable resistor R. The hardware is shown in Fig. 7.7 and the flowchart in Fig. 7.8

	LDA	#$00	Clear Control Register	A9	00	
	STA	$E001		8D	01	E0
	STA	$E000	Make data lines inputs?	8D	00	E0
	LDA	#$2C	Initialise CA2 neg-pulse output	A9	2C	
			CA1 flag active low without interr.			
	STA	$E001		8D	01	E0
SAMPLE	LDX	#$00	Clear X	A2	00	
	LDA	$E000	Dummy read of data register to			
			cause output pulse on CA2	AD	00	E0
TEST	BIT	$E001	Test for CA1 flag in control. If set,			
			N bit is set	2C	01	E0
	BMI	EXIT		30	03	
	INX			E8		
	BPL	TEST		10	F8	
EXIT	RTS		Returns with value in X	60		

The control register initialisation is shown above the dotted line in Program 29 and would, in practice, be part of the main program rather than within the body of the subroutine. The action is fairly straightforward. The X register grows (by incrementing) until the 555 timer output returns to the low state. This sets the flag because the initialisation programmed the flag to set when it detects a falling edge (active low). Once the flag is set, the subroutine returns to the calling program with the X register holding the binary equivalent of the resistor setting.

There will be a few practical hardware details to consider, such as the correct (or suitable) choice of capacitor and resistor value. The output pulse width of the 555 timer is 1.1 CR seconds. If CR is chosen too small, X will count up to maximum and overshoot before the flag is set. The value chosen must be adjusted to match the time it takes for X to

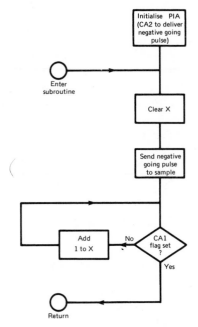

Fig. 7.8. Flowchart for program 29

count up to FF hex (255 decimal) when R is maximum. Examination of the TEST loop in Program 29 shows there are four instructions which, according to Appendix A, will occupy a time slice of twelve clock pulses per revolution. Assuming a 1 MHz clock, the loop will take approximately 3 ms to achieve maximum count in X. The product CR in the timer circuit must therefore be in this order of magnitude.

One final point regards voltages; the timer power supply must be 5 V to match the TTL levels of the PIA lines. It should be emphasised once more that coupling such equipment should only be undertaken if you are experienced in digital electronics. The 555 timer is cheap but the PIA output chip is not!

Interrupt action

Up to this point, care has been taken to avoid the CA1 flag causing an interrupt to occur by ensuring that bit 0 (the interrupt bit) in the control register is initialised to 0. It is time now to investigate what happens if this bit is set to 1.

It is advisable to re-read *Interrupt Signals* in Chapter 1 to refresh the details. On receipt of the CA1 (or CA2) signal which sets the appropriate flag, a signal called IRQ (interrupt request) is sent via the PIA up to the microprocessor. If the I bit in the processor status register is '0', the present program is interrupted and the computer jumps to a predetermined address and starts executing another program called the *Interrupt Service Routine*. On completion of this routine, the system returns to the original program and continues from the point at which it was interrupted. So much for the overall function; the application, however, is fraught with difficulty. In fact it should be pointed out that dabbling with the interrupt function in a home computer should be attempted with some reservations. It is a little difficult to write crashproof programs in which your own interrupt routines are interspersed because at all times you are competing with the operating system software which relies strongly on interrupt actions.

Before attempting to write interrupt routines, it is essential to examine the User's Manual to find the address of the interrupt request JUMP vector. There will be two locations holding this address in the usual low byte, high byte positions. The operating system will have already placed the address of its own 'private' routine in these addresses and it is essential that the contents are stored (preferably in the stack) before changing the contents to point at your own interrupt routine. You must also remember to restore the original contents at the end of the routine prior to returning from interrupt.

An interrupt may be defined as a peripheral-initiated subroutine, which implies that the program can have no knowledge of when the interrupt occurs. Fortunately it is in the nature of a *request* and, should the interrupt arrive at an inconvenient time, the request can be refused by strategic placing of the interrupt mask. Thus if a certain area of the main program is vulnerable and could not tolerate interruption (such as a critical timing loop or an initialisation routine) the interrupt mask SEI can be used at the beginning and cleared with CLI at the end. Should an interrupt request arrive within this area, it must wait passively until it reaches CLI.

An important thing to remember is that once an interrupt flag is set it will *remain* so until the data register is read. Failure to note this can sometimes be disastrous because once an interrupt is granted and the service routine entered, the system may immediately interrupt itself *ad infinitum*. The remedy of course is to insert a dummy read (say LDA E000) even if it is not wanted just to clear the interrupt flag.

Interrupt polling

If CA2 is an input then it too can be used under interrupt status. What happens if both of them arrive together? Furthermore, if an interrupt request is received how will the program know whether it was due to CA1 or CA2 peripheral? If the interrupt service routine is the same for both peripherals it doesn't really matter but this is unlikely. In most cases, the routine to service each peripheral would be different and therefore be located at different addresses. Referring back to Fig. 7.1 it will be seen that only *one* interrupt request line exists between the PIA and the microprocessor.

Thus there is no hardware distinction between CA1 and CA2 requests. The only way to ascertain from which input the request came is to check whether CA1 flag is set (bit 7) or CA2 flag (bit 6). This can be done by loading the control register and masking out the unwanted bits 0-5 or more economically by using the BIT test. Once the interrupt origin is established, the interrupt jump vector can be adjusted to point at the appropriate service routine address.

Why use interrupt?

There are two ways in which peripherals can be handled. One is the 'wait till ready' technique as illustrated in Program 29. Provided the entire system doesn't mind being tied up during the wait interval there is nothing gained by risking the perils of interrupt programming. Unfortunately, there will often be a requirement for some background program to run continuously, in which case using peripheral interruption at a strategic moment may be the only solution. It is obviously more economical and efficient to use interrupt procedures but it will be appreciated from the previous treatment that considerable experience is required before confidence in interrupt driven peripherals is gained.

The VIA (6522)

It was stated at the beginning of this chapter that the 6522, more commonly known as the VIA was a more complex version of the PIA. This was in essence true, although the differences are more in the form of additions or extra facilities rather than fundamental changes. Much of the preceding treatment of the PIA can be transferred without drastic modification to the VIA, particularly the programming of the direction and data registers. Before going into details perhaps the advantages or rather improvements over the PIA should be proudly presented.

In the first case, the annoying penny-pinching trick of two registers having to share the same address has been removed. Instead of using 'bit 2' in a control register to resolve address ambiguity, the VIA uses separate addresses for the data registers and the direction registers. Of course you never get anything for nothing; the VIA occupies sixteen addresses which indicates that there is a total of sixteen registers within the chip and directly programmable. The labelling employed in the VIA is different to the PIA. Fig. 7.9 shows the two halves, known as

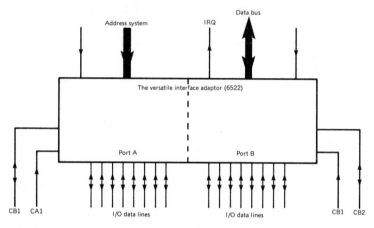

Fig. 7.9. VIA lines to the outside world

Port A and Port B. Each half contains eight data lines and two control lines. CA1 and CB1 can only be used as inputs while CA2 and CB2 can be used as either inputs or outputs depending on certain bits in the control register. As far as we have gone up to now, there is little difference to the PIA. However, when we consider the total register complement, it is excusable if a certain amount of gloom descends. In view of this, it is conducive to mental stability if they are atacked in a calm manner and only features of importance treated in any detail. We shall leave the complete register complement until later — it is frightening.

Continuing now with the major differences between the VIA and the PIA: Apart from the independent addressing of direction and data registers, perhaps the outstanding difference is the manner in which the control registers are organised. You may remember that a separate control register was used for each half of the PIA and the flag bits for the control lines CA1 and CA2 (and CB1, CB2) were situated in the control register. The VIA however departs from this scheme and uses only one control register, called the PCR or *Peripheral Control Register* to serve both halves. Since it is only the usual eight bits wide, only four

120

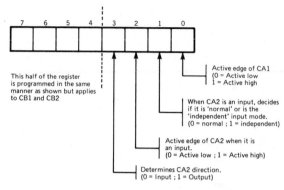

Fig. 7.10. The peripheral control register (assuming CA2 and CB2 are inputs)

bits are available for each half, bits 0–3 cater for Port A and bits 4–7 for Port B. Fig. 7.10 shows the allocation of the various bits, in detail for bits 0–3, although the left-hand half is identical (bit-position wise) for Port B. You will notice there are no flag bits because there is just no room for them. Instead, the VIA uses a separate register to handle the flag bits. It is eight bits wide so there is room for eight flags.

It is called the *Interrupt Flag Register* (IFR) and caters not only for the CA1, CA2, CB1 and CB2 flags but also for some powerful extra flags which belong to counters and shift registers etc. Fig. 7.11 shows the bit allocation although at this stage it would be better not to worry about

7	6	5	4	3	2	1	0
IRQ	T1	T2	CB1	CB2	SR	CA1	CA2

Bit	Set by	Cleared by
0	Active edge of CA2 (when input)	Reading or writing A port data
1	Active edge of CA1	Reading or writing A port data
2	Completion of 8 shifts	Reading or writing the shift register
3	Active edge of CB2 (when input)	Reading or writing the B port data
4	Active edge of CB1	Reading or writing the B port data
5	Timer 2 expired	Reading T2 low—order counter or writing T2 high—order counter
6	Timer 1 expired	Redaing T1 low—order counter or writing T1 high—order counter latch
7	An active and enabled interrupt state	Any action which clears the interrupt state

Fig. 7.11. The interrupt flag register (IFR)

the extras. Let us work our way through a simple exercise to illustrate the use of a control handshake by consulting Figs. 7.10 and 7.11.

Suppose we want to set a flag when the signal coming in on CA1 goes from low to high. We must ensure that bit 0 in the peripheral control register is first initialised with a '1' because this causes the CA1 flag to be set on an 'active high' signal. This will entail loading the pattern 01 hex into the accumulator first then storing it in the address at which the peripheral control register is situated (these addresses are discussed later). Subsequently, to find out whether or not a signal has arrived, we must examine the contents of the interrupt flag register to see if bit 1 is set. This, of course, can be achieved by the AND masking technique or alternatively by progressive shifting until the bit position is within the view of the 'test' instruction TST.

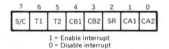

1 = Enable interrupt
0 = Disable interrupt

When bit 7 is 1   Any remaining bits at 1 are set to 1
When bit 7 is 0   Any remaining bits at 1 are set to 0
(Any remaining bits at 0 have no effect)

Fig. 7.12. The interrupt enable register (IER)

Now for another discrepancy between the PIA and the VIA. When a flag is set you may or may not require an interrupt request to be sent up the IRQ line to the microprocessor. In the PIA, you will remember that bits were allocated in the control register for this purpose. In the VIA, again an entirely separate register is allocated called the *Interrupt Enable Register* (IER) and is shown in Fig. 7.12. If you fail to understand this figure you should not feel humble — it frightened me to start with and still does.

Let's try an example with the following scenario.

Assume that when CB1 flag is set we wish an interrupt to be enabled which of course means sending a signal up the IRQ line. At the same time, any existing interrupts are to be disabled. This is what we could do:

```
LDA     $6F
STA     IER     Place the pattern 01101111 in the interrupt enable
                register to clear any existing bits except the CB1 bit
LDA     $90
STA     IER     Place the pattern 10010000 in the IER to confirm that
                CB1 is to interrupt.
```

The first operation is to disable unwanted interrupts which is why bit 7 was a 0. The next operation contains a 1 in bit 7 which confirms the interrupt status of bit 4 (the CB1 position).

It may be of interest to note that the two patterns are the one's complement of each other. You will of course appreciate that it was possible for several interrupts (or rather flags) to be set at any one time because peripherals may barge in, with no manners, at any time. It will be up to you to clobber them until such time as you are ready to deal with them.

Before tackling the counter and timer registers, another example, consolidating previous work, may be useful. As in the previous example, symbolic addresses will be used.

Example.   Initialise (configurate) the VIA to behave as follows:
Port A to be all inputs. Port B to be all outputs. CA1 to be active high input which is to enable the interrupt. CA2, CB1 and CB2 to be active high inputs without interrupt.
To make head and tail of the following you should have Figs. 7.10, 7.11, and 7.12 in mind.

```
LDA   #$00
STA      Port A   Port A all inputs
LDA   #$FF
STA      Port B   Port B all outputs
LDA   #$55
STA      PCR      Place 01010101 in peripheral control register (CA1,
                  CA2, CB1, CB2 active high inputs at 'normal' mode
LDA   #$7D
STA      IER      Place 01111101 in interrupt enable register to disable
                  all interrupts except CA1
LDA   #$82
STA      IER      Place 10000010 in interrupt enable register to confirm
                  interrupt enable on CA1
```

Some explanation is required at this point concerning the term 'normal' mode above. Referring to Fig. 7.10 again note that bit 1 decides this. It refers to the method you choose for resetting the CA2 flag when it is an *input.* Under 'normal' mode CA2 flag remains set until it is reset by programming a 0 into the interrupt flag register. This choice allows CA2 (or CB2) to be used as an isolated input control if desired.

You may be wondering at this stage whether or not it is worth carrying on or is there already sufficient complexity to keep your personality subdued for ever. Remember that the previous work is hard and demands much practice before it begins to sink in. The VIA is very sophisticated — in fact I think it is a work of genius and the designers deserve the Nobel Prize for chips. Unfortunately, works of genius demand a genius to understand them *easily.* Now follows the rest of the contraption — best of luck!

Fig. 7.10 showed the meaning of each bit in the peripheral control register on the assumption than bit 3 was a 0, thus making CA2 an Input. (Similarly bit 7 at 0 would make CB2 an input.) If bit 3 however is set to 1, the picture changes and we must now examine Fig. 7.13.

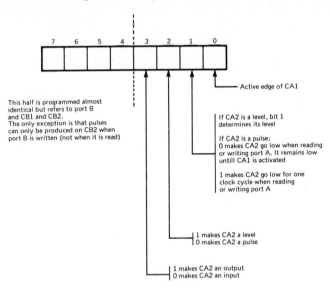

Fig. 7.13. The peripheral control register (assuming CA2 and CB2 are outputs)

In the first place, bit 3 must be 1 (and bit 7 for the B side). You then have a choice of the kind of output you want on CA2. This can either be a simple 'level' output in which case it assumes the same state at bit 1.

Example. Suppose you want CA2 to behave as a level then the right hand half must be set with the pattern:
110X for CA2 to remain at 0
111X for CA2 to remain at 1
(The 'X' above is irrelevant to this issue because it belongs to CA1 active level.)

Clearly, you must keep changing bit 1 every time you wish to change the state of CA2.

Example. Suppose you want to produce a negative-going pulse (high to low and back again) on CA2 output.
The pattern in the right hand half must now be 101X.

124

When subsequently you require such an output pulse, it is only necessary to perform a dummy read or write on the A Port.

The auxiliary control register and the timer/counters

This is yet another register to worry about if (and only if) you want to experiment with the timers. It is shown in Fig. 7.14 and you will note that bit 7 and bit 6 are concerned with timer 1 and bits 2, 3 and 4 are concerned with shift register functions. Timer 1 is very complicated and usually tied up by the operating system of a personal computer so we shall leave it alone. The shift register can be used for serial to parallel conversion and vice versa but is not often used so we shall leave this alone as well.

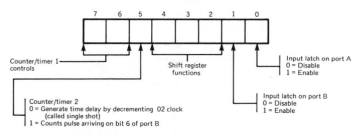

Fig. 7.14. The auxiliary control register (ACR)

This leaves one timer for us to discuss, timer 1 which is handled by bit 5 in the auxiliary control register. Before treating this, let's get the two right-hand bits out of the way. You will note from Fig. 7.14 that bit 0 and bit 1 refer to 'input latches' and are nothing whatsoever to do with timer functions. Indeed, they belong to the data ports.

Input latches

The term 'latch' has been described earlier but in this sense we can consider them as *holding* registers. When Port A or Port B are used as *outputs,* the latching is inherent. That is to say, any data loaded in to them *remains* there until it is subsequently changed by a fresh load operation. When these ports are used as *inputs,* the incoming data is normally fed raw to the input registers of the ports and can be continually changing. If, however, it is required to sample the input data at some definate time, the current input can be latched in by an active signal on CA1 for Port A or CB1 for Port B.

Either or both ports can be operated under latched conditions by writing '1's in bit 0 or bit 1 positions of the auxiliary control register. Once input data has been latched, the data coming in is ignored until it required to relatch.

Timer 2

Timer 2 is virtually a 16-bit counter and occupies two addresses, low-byte and high-byte. Once a number is loaded into the counter (low order byte first) it is automatically decremented down to 0 by either

(a) the clock pulses of the microcomputer (if single shot mode is used)
or
(b) incoming pulses from an external device on to *pin 6 of Port B* (this will take precedence over normal Port B actions).

The time finishes when the count reaches zero, at which time the timer 2 flag is set (bit 5 in the interrupt flag register (refer back to Fig. 7.11). Thus we can use these facilities for producing a *simple time delay* in terms of (N) clock pulses or we can use them to count the number of external events which have occurred.

Example. Produce a time delay of 2560 (hex) clock pulses.

LDA	#$00	
STA	ACR	Ensure one shot mode is established in the auxiliary control register (bit 5 = 0)
LDA	#$60	
STA	T2L	Store low-order counter
LDA	#$25	
STA	T2H	Store high-byte counter (timing interval now starts automatically)
LDA	$2D	Produce mask to check timer 2 flag (00100000)
BACK BIT	IFR	Is flag set in interrupt flag register
BEQ	BACK	Not yet
LDA	T2L	Reading the timer 2 low-byte resets the flag.

Example. Cont external pulses arriving on pin 6 of Port B until 200 have arrived.

LDA	#$00	
STA	DRB	Make Port B inputs (by clearing direction register)
LDA	#$20	
STA	ACR	Ensure timer 2 is in pulse-counting mode (Bit 5 = 1 in auxiliary control register)

```
        LDA   #$00
        STA   T2L        Store low-order counter
        LDA   #$20
        STA   T2H        Store high-order counter (count now ready)
        LDA   #$20       Mask for timer 2 flag (00100000)
BACK    BIT   IFR        Timer 2 flag set yet?
        BEQ   BACK       Not yet
        LDA   T2L        Reading T2 low-order byte resets flag.
```

Apart from listing the address order for the individual registers of the VIA, that about covers all we have space for.

Relative address	VIA register
XXX0	Output register for port B
XXX1	Output register for port A
XXX2	Port B direction register
XXX3	Port A direction register
XXX4	Timer 1 counter low—order byte
XXX5	Timer 1 counter high—order byte
XXX6	Timer 1 latch low—order byte
XXX7	Timer 1 latch high—order byte
XXX8	Timer 2 counter low—order byte
XXX9	Timer 2 counter high—order byte
XXXA	Serial shift register
XXXB	Auxiliary control register
XXXC	Peripheral control register
XXXD	Interrupt flag register
XXXE	Interrupt enable register
XXXF	Output register for port A (no handshaking)

Fig. 7.15. VIA address allocations

The addresses are shown in Fig. 7.15 and are always in this sequence, i.e., occupying *consecutive addresses*. The *absolute* addresses of course will depend on your manual which will (or should) give you a memory map which includes the VIA residence block.

Summary

- Peripherals are slow and almost always asynchronous.
- Peripherals must be both hardware and software interfaced to the computer input/output chip.
- There are two popular input/output chips used with the 6502. They are the PIA (6520) and the VIA (6522).
- The PIA has two halves. Each half supports eight data lines and two handshake lines. All lines are TTL compatible.

- The VIA is similar to the PIA but contains extra shift and counter facilities.
- The PIA is memory mapped and the assumed addresses for example purposes have been E000 and E001.
- The direction register contents determine which data lines are outputs and which are inputs. Bits at 1 are outputs; bits at 0 are inputs.
- The data register contents are reflected in the data lines.
- Data and direction registers share the same address E000.
- The control register is at address E001. Bit 2 in this register determines which of the two registers is selected; if bit 2 is 0, the direction register is addressed, if bit 2 is 1 the data register is addressed.
- Under RESET conditions, all PIA registers are filled with '0's.
- Data lines programmed to behave as inputs will not accept data from the data register.
- CA1 is always an input. CA2 can be an input or an output depending on bit in the control register. If bit 5 is 1, CA2 is an output.
- CA1 and CA2 (when an input) are 'edge triggered' inputs. On detection of the correct edge a flag bit is set in the control register. CA1 flag is bit 7, CA2 flat is bit 6.
- Once a flag is set, it can only be reset by reading the data register.
- The vunerable edge of CA1 depends on bit 1 in the control register. If bit 1 is 0, the falling edge sets the flag. If 1, a rising edge sets the flag. When CA2 is an input, bit 4 determines the vulnerable edge.
- When a flag is set, it may or may not send out an interrupt request (IRQ) to the microprocessor. The decision depends on bit 0 for CA1 and bit 3 for CA2. The behaviour of CA2 as an output depends on bits 3 and 4 in the control register.
- Although the external interface wires of the VIA are identical to the PIA, it is a more complex chip with many additional features.
- There are 16 registers each occupying separate addresses on the memory map.
- The peripheral control register is eight bits wide and is functionally in two identical halves which serve the A and B port control lines respectively.
- The interrupt flag register houses the four flags for CA1, CA2, CB1 and CB2 inputs and flags for the timers and the shift register. One of the bits is dedicated to interrupt enable/disable.
- The interrupt enable register is used in conjunction with the seven flag bits to determine which is to send an interrupt request.
- The control line CA2 has a unique capability. It can be set in the 'normal' mode (flag reset automatically on a read or write of Port A)

or the 'independent' mode (flag reset only by direct resetting by a '0'). The mode is established by bit 1 in the peripheral control register.

● There are two programmable timers, timer 1 and timer 2. Each of these is 16 bits long and therefore occupy two addresses each (low byte and high byte).

● Timer 2 is usually available to the user and can be used as a time delay or to count the number of external events. Depending on the number set into the timer during initialisation, a predictable time elapses before the number is counted down to zero. When this happens, the appropriate flag is set.

● The auxiliary control register is used to control timer 1, timer 2, a shift register and the input latches on Port A and Port B.

● The shift register can be used for parallel serial transformations.

● The 16 addresses allocated to the VIA must always be in numerical sequence XXX0 to XXXF hex. Apart from the extra registers mentioned, there are two direction registers and two data output registers.

8

Static and dynamic graphics

Background hardware

Information can be presented on the screen face in two distinct ways. Firstly in the form of normal printed text and secondly in the form of 'pictures'. Machines vary in their capability of portraying pictures, depending on such factors as memory, or rather the amount of memory dedicated to the screen map, and the *pixel* size. A pixel may be defined as the number of dots which, treated as a packet of information, have a uniquely addressable location. Two kinds of machines may be recognised:

Low resolution graphics
Those in which the pixel size is equal to the area required to portray a textual character. Such a pixel would typically be an 8 × 8 matrix of dots making 64 in all. Pictures, or to use the less 'picturesque' term *graphics,* would be crude and lacking in resolution, equivalent to using a distemper brush as the drawing instrument. The pictures which are used in the CEEFAX or ORACLE texts are typical of this *low-resolution* graphical system. The effect is similar to children's building bricks.

High resolution graphics
Facilities exist for dissecting out smaller parts of the 8 × 8 character matrix, sometimes even down to a single dot. Thus each dot or a group of perhaps four or six dots can be individually addressed which means that pictures can be drawn in finer detail — the artist's small camel hair brush rather than the distemper brush.

A machine designed for low resolution graphics *only* can never be upgraded by software techniques either in high level or machine code instructions. The resolution capability is hardware dictated during the design stage.

Fig. 8.1 illustrates the kind of hardware used to provide normal text characters. Most of the work is performed by a chip which is virtually a ROM containing all the bits necessary to light up the VDU in the right places for each individual character. The chip is known as the *Character Generator* and may contain either 64 character or 128 character fonts

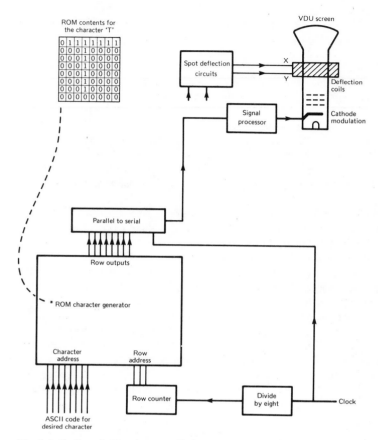

Fig. 8.1. Outline of video character display system

(the term 'font' means the dot matrix pattern used to present the character visually). The inset in Fig. 8.1 shows how the upper case 'T' is stored in the ROM and assumes that a logic 1 causes the screen to light up and a logic 0 to appear black. Although it is not strictly necessary for a machine code programmer to understand the intricacies of Fig. 8.1 it will help in gaining an overall understanding. The diagram is simplified of course and contains only sufficient detail for a preliminary understanding. The ROM which stores the characters has two addressing systems:

The character address

The ASCII code for the desired character is presented at these inputs and selects the particular 8×8 matrix. For example, the

ASCII code for upper case 'T' is 84 (decimal) or 54 (hex) so the binary pattern present on the character address inputs would be 01010100.

The row address

A cathode ray tube must have the input information fed *serially* onto a single electrode called the *cathode*. This means that the 84 bits which form a given character must somehow be stretched out so that only one dot at a time is presented to the cathode. This stretching process is achieved in two steps, the first step is carried out by the *row address* which appears on the three input wires. Three wires can give any of the eight combinations from 000 to 111. Each combination selects *one row* of eight which appears at the *row output* wires.

The second step of the stretching process is carried out by the *parallel to serial converter*. This is a simple logic chip which accepts the eight bits parallel input and on the receipt of clock pulses, feeds them out one at a time. The output, which is normal TTL or CMOS logic, is now processed in order to satisfy the special requirements of the tube cathode. A logic 1 must be made to light up the tube which means that it must be converted to a negative-going step by the signal processor.

After each row is converted, the *row counter* is incremented to bring the next row into operation which is then converted to serial as before. Thus to present a complete character requires conversion of all eight rows before the 64 dots are completely disgorged into the tube cathode. This is a lengthy process to describe and it may appear strange that steady characters can be visible on the screen almost instantaneously. We must realise however that electronic speeds more than make up for the inherent complexity of such a drawn out process. The dots are presented at a speed of less than a microsecond per dot and together with the obliging characteristic of the human eye to retain images help to present a nice illusion.

The details of the synchronisation process and the sordid details of the tube scanning circuits must be left to your imagination although it will be appreciated that a frightening amount of complexity must be built in to the system. The tube is scanned into a television raster which causes the spot to sweep from left to right to generate each line and from top to bottom to complete each 'frame'.

It should be mentioned that not all systems use an 8×8 matrix for the character font. Some use only a 7×5 while others use 9×8. Clearly, the more dots used to portray a character, the more pleasing to the eye is that character.

There is one other piece of electronic wizardry to explain regarding the problem of keeping the screen steady whilst the computer is carrying out other sundry tasks. This problem is solved by our old friend 'interrupt'. The resident operating system arranges that every 1/50th of a second the current operation carried out is interrupted and the screen is repainted. Thus there will be an interrupt service routine which carries out this operation. The human eye cannot respond to images which are changed more rapidly that about twentyfive times per second so the current picture appears to be stationary.

Graphic keys

Some microcomputers have key legends which provide an alternative character set allowing diagrams to be built up. The characters occupy the same dot matrix space as ordinary text but instead of letters and numbers they paint lines and squiggles. The effect is pleasing, considering it is still low resolution, although a second best in comparison with more ambitious systems using true high-resolution graphics. Because of the extra character set, graphic keys often carry the penalty of non-standardised keyboards which can be annoying for those used to the standard Qwerty layout. Very often, the inclusion of graphic keys carries a further penalty because the ASCII code for screen graphics would encroach on the normal text character space. This leads to an additional set (called the POKE code) for characters originating from the screen memory. It is probable that graphic keys will gradually be phased out in future home computers as high resolution graphic capabilities may soon become the norm.

Fig. 8.2. Quadrant graphics keys

There are certain novel but inefficient ways in which it is possible to double the effective X and Y resolution on those machines which include graphics keys as shown in Fig. 8.2. These keys divide the normal full character matrix into quadrants and by careful programming, which includes the AND and OR techniques, can effectively pick out each separate quadrant. However, to call this trick 'high-resolution graphics' is debatable.

Graphics software

We shall discuss only the coding for machines which are restricted to low resolution graphics, that is, those in which the pixel size is the text character size. (The coding for high-resolution graphics would be in essence the same but would be very much more dependent on individual machine characteristics.)

PEEK and POKE analogies

Those used to programming games or other projects involving moving graphics in BASIC will be familiar with the keywords POKE and PEEK and they will also be aware of the underlying hazards in their use. POKE and PEEK operations have caused more machine crashes than any other BASIC keyword. The reason, of course, is that these two operations although part of high-level BASIC are functionally in a grey area, halfway between high-level and machine code. Thus the operation POKE 120, A will store the contents of the variable 'A' into the machine address 120, the address of course taken to mean the *decimal* address (BASIC seldom allows the interpretation of hexadecimal to variables). POKEing obviously overrides the protective cloak of the resident operating system and, in the example quoted, would possibly (or rather *probably* since the address is in page one) cause a machine crash. However, most POKEing operations would in practice be carried out on the area of memory dedicated to the screen, in which case the results of a miscalculation in address would be irritating rather than catastrophic.

It is a good plan to approach machine code graphics by linking the operations mentally with PEEK and POKE — approaching the unknown from the known philosophy!

Thus POKE 120, 12 in BASIC will correspond to:

        LDA 0C   (12 decimal is 0C hex)
        STA 78   (120 decimal is 78 hex)

It will be seen that POKE in BASIC requires two separate machine code operations, one to place the pattern in the accumulator and another to store it in the desired memory location.

PEEK on the other hand is more simple and can be considered in machine code as a single operation.

Thus the operation:

        A = PEEK (65) will correspond (crudely) with:
        LDA 41 (Decimal 65 is 41 hex)

It is appreciated of course that the variable 'A' in BASIC is floating point but this only effects the *destination* of the PEEKed result. The desination of the machine code example could have been the X or Y register by using LDX or LDY respectively.

Background graphics

Graphics in general and computer games in particular require two kinds of display, the stationary background and the moving (dynamic) object or objects. The background picture poses no problems but can be full of tedium both in high level language and machine code. It will consist of a painstaking exercise of placing particular characters in particular addresses so that the overall effect is one of a pictorial representation of say a landscape.

The particular graphic used to build up the picture can be the asterisk* or in the case of graphic key availability, any of the special curves and squiggles. Fig. 8.3 shows a simple 'background' assumed to be in the bottom half of the screen and composed entirely of * characters.

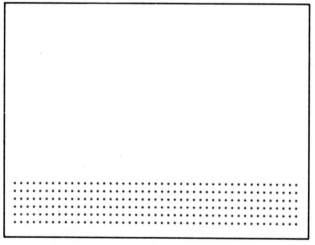

Fig. 8.3. Background graphics example

Continuing our policy of relating machine code to the equivalent BASIC, let us first program using PEEK codes to form such a background. We assume that the machine allows 40 characters per line so to build up the background of six lines would require a loop causing 6 × 40 = 240 asterisks to be POKED into the appropriate area within the screen map.

135

Assuming the ASCII code is used for the asterisks (42 decimal, 2A hex) and the address of the top left * is (for simplicity) a nice round figure of 8000 hex or 32768 decimal, the BASIC code could take this form:

```
10000 S = 32768: REM START OF DESIRED BACKGROUND
10010 FOR N = 0 to 239
10020 POKE S + N, 42
10030 NEXT N
10040 RETURN
```

The equivalent machine code version might take the following form:

Program 30

	LDA	#$2A	Hex code for ``*''	A9	2A	
	LDX	#$00	Clear X	A2	00	
BACK	STA	8000, X	Top of loop to store ``*''	8D	00	80
	INX			E8		
	CPX	#$F0	Test for 240 (decimal) revs	E0	F0	
	BNE	BACK		D0	F8	
	RTS			60		

Since this is a subroutine it would be wise to consider a more universal form in which the starting address of the screen and the ASCII code to be implanted could be left undetermined; that is left to the responsibility of the calling program. Thus the accumulator contents could be assumed and indexed indirect addressing could be used in place of the simple indexed form. This of course means that the calling program can, by loading the appropriate screen address bytes in the indirect address, choose which part of the screen is to receive the background program.

The following is the alternative arrangement using symbolic addresses:

Program 31

	LDY	#$00	Clear Y	A0	00	
BACK	STA	(SCREEN),				
		Y	'SCREEN' must be address where			
			lower order byte is assumed.			
			SCREEN + 1 must contain high			
			order byte	91	xx	xx
	INY			C8		
	CPY	#$F0	End of loop test	C0	F0	
	BNE	BACK		D0	F8	
	RTS			60		

136

Backgrounds built up by painting the same character on the screen are easiest to program but are obviously restricted in artistic content. Unfortunately, to widen the scope to include mixtures of any desired character demands a tedious placing of the ASCII (or POKE code) in a data list at the end of the program — or other safe memory block.

A convenient system where data lists are concerned is to ensure the *first* item in the list is not a character code but is simply the *number* of codes (data items) to follow. This number can then be used in the 'end of test' comparison in the loop which activates the list.

Let us assume for purposes of illustration that such a list is resident at machine hex addresses 1000 onwards and contains 240 (decimal) items, the first item would then be F0 hex. the data items would thus reside in hex addresses 1001 to 10F1 inclusive. The program segment would take the following form:

Program 32

	LDY	#$00	Clear Y	A0	00	
BACK	LDY	1001, Y	Load data item from list	B9	01	10
	STA	(SCREEN),				
		Y	Index indirect as before	91	xx	xx
	INY	C8				
	CPY	1000	Compares Y with absolute address contents of first item in list			
	BNE	BACK		D0	F4	
	RTS			60		

Note that the Y register is used both for sequencing through the data list using absolute indexed addressing and again for the indexed indirect mode for painting the characters onto the SCREEN area.

The superior speed of machine code over BASIC is well confirmed in these examples. It is far better visually to see a background appear virtually instantaneous rather than the slow character by character sweep of most BASICs.

Dynamic graphics

How do we make an object 'move' across the background using machine code? It is probable that most readers are already familiar with the method used in BASIC and there is no revolutionary method of implementing the effect using machine code. It might be profitable, as in the last example, to approach the problem via BASIC in the first instance in order to more easily follow the mchine code equivalent.

We shall consider the 'object' to be moved is a single character such as the * although the letter O provides a reasonable ball for game simulation. The principle is as follows, assuming the ball is to progress from left to right:

1. Display the ball at screen address A.
2. Hold it there for a reasonable time interval.
3. Erase the ball with a 'space' or blank.
4. Display the ball at screen address A + 1.
5. Test for ball hitting boundary of screen.
6. If test is NO, jump back to 1.

The speed of travel will depend on the delay used in line 2 although in machines which have a slow BASIC system, the inherent machine delay may in itself be more than sufficient without employing a delay subroutine. If the ball is to be moved from right to left, the A + 1 in line 4 is replaced by A—1.

The following code is designed to make the object move from left to right. The delay to hold the ball is assumed to be supplied by a simple delay subroutine which of course must be *in situ* before running.

Program 33

	LDY	#20	ASCII code for space	A0	20	
	LDX	#00	Clear X for character count	A2		
BACK	LDA	1000	Code for ball assumed in this address, (*) would do	AD	00	10
	STA	SCREEN, X	Display object	9D	xx	xx
	JSR	DELAY	Hold displayed object	20	xx	xx
	TYA		Acc now holds space code	98		
	STA	SCREEN, X	Object rendered invisible	9D	xx	xx
	INX			E8		
	CPX	#27	Test for end of line	E0	27	
	BNE	BACK		D0	EE	
	RTS			60		

The above assumes a line length of 40 characters occupying columns 0 to 39 decimal (00 to 27 hex). The screen address has again been left as a symbolic operand.

If the object of the dynamic display is to cause the object to impact on a target or a boundary line, it is a simple matter to test the contents of the next character position. If this is a code for 'space' the object can continue its flight; if not, the boundary is reached and appropriate action can follow depending on the game's strategy.

High-resolution graphics

It would be an exercise of doubtful value to give examples of machine code which act upon high-resolution modes since the facilities are specific to the resident machine operating system. Unfortunately the high-res graphics area has grown up in piecemeal fashion. Because of the compexity involved (and the tedium) it is probably the best idea to use the many existing machine code subroutines which handle the graphics. There is little point in re-inventing the wheel. Even if you are a purist and normally scorn the work of others there is still an opportunity to display originality in the manner in which you string these subroutines together. All you need is the listing of the machine code version of the BASIC interpreter and the operating system. There are many enterprising writers who have dug out this information on the various popular machines — not all manufacturers are forthcoming in this area.

Mention should be made here of the superb high-resolution graphic facilities on the BBC/ACORN machine which, because of the machine code subroutines which abound, are particularly relevant to this subject. ACORN have always been inclined towards rather low level programming and love interspersing machine parameters with their BASIC keywords. Although the BASIC is in general close to the popular and well known MICROSOFT standard, some very powerful extras are included, particularly in the field of high-resolution graphics and colour. There is a particularly powerful keyword 'VDU' which is a general-purpose instruction to access the graphics systems. The keyword is followed by a string of separate parameters which are almost of pure machine code breed and therefore very fast in execution.

9

General guidelines

A book of this size can do little more than present the instruction code of the 6502 and describe the function and possible application of each separate code. It is doubtful whether a book of any size can literally teach you how to program. Programming in a high level language like BASIC is an intellectual *exercise* but programming in machine code is more of an intellectual *battle* because in the early stages of acquiring the art you get the distinct impression the machine is hostile. It is so easy to become frustrated and return to the relatively friendly environment of BASIC. The great thing is not to expect too much too early and above all, don't attempt to write ambitious programs until you have tried out simple little routines for several weeks or even months. This chapter is devoted to the pitfalls of machine code, a kind of 'aid for frustrated programmers'.

Correct mental attitude

Approach the machine with compassion not anger. Remember the poor old 6502 (or indeed any other microprocessor) has extremely limited mental powers and cannot understand the complex orders we take for granted when conversing with the help of a BASIC interpreter. Machine code instructions are *atoms* of action not molecules — we are not even building with bricks as a starting point because the bricks themselves must first be fashioned out of sand and clay. A pessimistic but sound philosophy to adopt in the early stages is as follows:

> Programs written in BASIC seldom work first time, machine code programs never do.

With this attitude of mind you will never be frustrated and occasionally (very occasionally) you will be pleasantly surprised.

Before sitting at the keyboard

It is a common habit with BASIC to compose a program at the

140

keyboard in spite of the textbook advice against it. It is understandable why this advice is ignored because it is so easy in BASIC to write a few lines and then give it a quick whirl to see if it works. If it doesn't, the syntax or other errors are corrected and it is tried again. In fact the ease of correction and modification is probably the main reason for the popularity of BASIC or indeed any *interpreted* rather than *compiled* high-level language. Programs can be built up piecemeal fashion by repeated bouts of trial and error. Any attempt to adopt similar techniques in machine code programming is doomed to failure.

Never compose machine code at the keyboard. Always work it out on paper first in a tidy format and avoid scribbling and masses of alterations. Always use a pencil (never ink) in the provisional draft because errors are the rule not the exception.

Never trust to your memory for hex machine codes — even if you are certain about the code *look it up* in Appendix 1. Just think of the havoc if you wrote 9A instead of A9! If you have an assembler then looking up the codes will not be a problem although another possible hazard will be an incorrect operand symbol. Instead of the machine codes you will always require that part of the user manual which deals with the assembler format. Remember that the assembler symbolism used in this book is not necessarily valid in your micro — hex codes are always the same for the 6502 but assembly language is subject to makers' variations.

Entering at the keyboard

It is important to be methodical when entering machine code. BASIC almost encourages slap-happy keyboard work because of the editing facilities built-in to the language; it is so easy to correct errors after running. Machine code monitors in most microcomputers are lacking in friendliness and offer virtually no help. In all fairness to the system designer of a typical home computer, machine code programming is assumed to be unpopular with the majority of users and it is considered uneconomical to devote too much ROM space to a monitor. Very few makes include assemblers in the resident software although the ACORN and the BBC micro are exceptional in this respect.

It is a good plan to SAVE your machine code program on tape *before* you try the first RUN because of the very real danger of a system crash. It is ridiculously easy to crash the machine with a faulty machine code program. Even a wrong address, a wrong code or entering the program in a forbidden area of RAM can result in loss of keyboard control. No damage of course but the program must be re-entered again from scratch, an exercise not conducive to tranquillity. If you SAVE first and then RUN, at least you have a fall-back version to re-enter if the machine does crash on the first (or thirteenth) attempt.

It is possible, if your machine provides the POKE function in BASIC, to be independent of the monitor and POKE the machine code program via a DATA/READ loop. This provides no additional saveguard against a machine crash. In fact, your first experience of a crash whilst still in BASIC was probably due to POKEing.

Curing bugs

Curing bugs is easy. Finding them can lead to anguish. In some cases, it feels rather like trying to find a non-existent black cat in a dark room. There are so many reasons for a program failure that it is difficult to formulate a logical fault-finding procedure — in practice it is usually the last thing you try! In order of *probability*, the following is as good a sequence as any.

Incorrectly entered

It is easy to either mistype a line or to leave one out completely because machine code is literally *coded* language and therefore mistakes are not obvious. Examine every character entered against the paper copy otherwise you will spend a fruitless hour or so trying to find a non-existent bug.

Entered in the wrong block of RAM

As mentioned several times before, the space free for machine codes in the memory map is restricted to certain address blocks. Even if the program itself is absolutely correct, its presence in a reserved area can kill the operating system or the BASIC interpreter. Check again that your code is legitimately located. Even if the coding *starts* in a harmless area, it may be of such a length that it extends across into forbidden territory. Remember it is usually possible to annexe the BASIC area by use of HIMEM (if you have it) or, by consulting the manual, POKEing a new number in an address pointer.

Program overlapping the data

When a program is first scribbled out on paper it is seldom known with any degree of precision how many bytes it will occupy, so locations earmarked for holding *data* which the program is to use are chosen provisionally in the first instance. Very often, the program length is underestimated and there is a danger that the program will eat up its own data because it is *within* rather than at the *end* of the program. In the case of assembly language, the danger is often minimised because a common facility is automatic location of data at the end of the program lines. There is of course no necessity for data bytes to be at the end of a program; they could just as well be placed before the head.

Relative address error

Conditional branch instructions use *relative* addressing which means that when in machine code without the help of an assembler, you have to count the bytes backwards or forwards. Backward branches are particularly error prone because of the need to convert to two's complement notation. Consider the havoc caused by being just one count out when calculating a relative address. In most cases, this will cause a branch to an *operand* instead of an Op Code which of course the microprocessor will attempt to execute. It would be pure chance if the result of an operand 'code' turned out to be benign.

Incorrect addressing mode

There are eight different LDAs, eight different ADCs and so on. It is easy to make an error in an addressing mode. A particularly error prone example is indirect indexed and indexed indirect mix up! Don't forget that only the X register is used in indexed indirect and only the Y register in indirect indexed.

Two byte operands back to front

It is a pity from the human viewpoint that two byte operands must be written back to front in 6502 code. This means that the normal human tendency to enter the address 0600 hex as 0600 is, as far as the 6502 is concerned 'back to front'. We should not blame the 6502 for this quirk because it is more efficient from the hardware viewpoint if it sees the lower order byte *first*.

False assumptions

Never assume the carry bit is '0' before an addition and never assume it is '1' before a subtraction. Likewise never assume there is plenty of room left in the stack. It is usually a simple matter to check the contents of the stack pointer to see if it is dangerously near 01FF hex (the last free location in the stack).

Incorrect branch code

If for example you have chosen BPL, are you certain you wish to branch if positive? Don't forget that zero is a positive number and can easily cause an unexpected result. Another common cause of error is the interpretation of a double negative when using BNE. For example if the 'yes' branch is followed, remember that this really means 'yes, it is *not equal*' which is an unhappy piece of gobbledegook and easily misinterpreted in a flowchart.

Errors of logic

As a last resort, if none of the previous suggestions help, the flowchart (if there is one) should be re-examined. It is customary in some circles to construct a rough outline flowchart first and then a more detailed

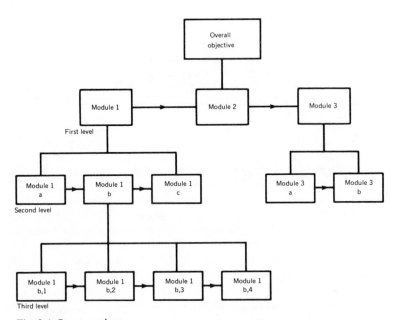

Fig. 9.1. Structure chart

version. In fact the traditional flowchart layout is often abandoned in favour of a 'structure chart' which portrays more effectively the various levels of detail. Fig. 9.1 illustrates the idea behind such a chart. Unlike a conventional flowchart, in which the flow is from top to bottom, the structure chart is read horizontally from left to right. The horizontal row beneath a given row is merely a more detailed version. If an error of logic exists, such a structure allows a more organised search to proceed.

However, it is not easy to give advice or suggest rules how to find errors of logic. Very often, if the bugs resist repeated attempts, it may often pay to cut your losses by scrapping the project and starting again from a fresh angle. Don't be ashamed if you have to resort to this apparently degrading act — I never am.

Using existing subroutines

Lurking within the bowels of the resident BASIC interpreter will be found many useful machine code subroutines. These will have been written by experts and thoroughly debugged before they were allowed to enter the ROM. By splicing them into your own code you will be spared routine tasks irksome to write but nevertheless essential. For example, a subroutine to get a character entered from the keyboard and place it in the accumulator can be a recurring need.

To use these subroutines it is necessary to:

1. Know the starting address of the required routine. This information may be in an appendix to the User's Manual but very often it will require a trip to the local computer shop for a book dealing with the detailed anatomy of your model. Fortunately, there are many enterprising writers who, with dogged determination, manage to ferret out all those bits of information which *should* be in the manual but are not.
2. Know the *calling* procedures. Subroutines assume that certain parameters have been lodged in certain registers so it is essential these are loaded prior to using JSR.

Using other people's subroutines may be considered cheating if, that is, you have an idealistic temperament. Even if you do not use them, it is worth while examining the listings in order to stimulate ideas for later use. Programming, particularly in machine code, has grown up bit by bit over the years and all the common subroutines such as floating point addition, multiplication and division are the result of a communal mind and hence 'public domain' category.

Appendix 1
6502 machine code summary

Alphabetical list of op code mnemonics

	Action in 'words'	*Action in 'operational symbolism'*
ADC	Add with carry	$A + M + C \rightarrow A$
AND	Logical AND	$A \wedge M \rightarrow A$
ASL	Arithmetic shift left	$C \leftarrow \boxed{} \leftarrow 0$
BCC	Branch if carry clear	Branch if $C = 0$
BCS	Branch if carry set	Branch if $C = 1$
BEQ	Branch if equal	Branch if $Z = 1$
BIT	Bit test	$M7 \rightarrow N$; $M6 \rightarrow V$; $A \wedge M$ and update Z
BMI	Branch if minus	Branch if $N = 1$
BNE	Branch if not equal	Branch if $Z = 0$
BPL	Branch if plus	Branch if $N = 0$
BRK	Break	$PC = PC + 1$
BVC	Branch if overflow clear	Branch if $V = 0$
BVS	Branch if overflow set	Branch if $V = 1$
CLC	Clear carry	$0 \rightarrow C$
CLD	Clear decimal mode	$0 \rightarrow D$
CLI	Clear interrupt mask	$0 \rightarrow I$
CLV	Clear overflow	$0 \rightarrow V$
CMP	Compare with accumulator	$A - M$ and update N, Z and C
CPX	Compare with X register	$X - M$ and update N, Z and C
CPY	Compare with Y register	$Y - M$ and update N, Z and C
DEC	Decrement memory	$M - 1 \rightarrow M$
DEX	Decrement X register	$X - 1 \rightarrow X$
DEY	Decrement Y register	$Y - 1 \rightarrow Y$
EOR	Logical EXCLUSIVE OR	$A \veebar M \rightarrow A$
INC	Increment memory	$M + 1 \rightarrow M$
INX	Increment X register	$X + 1 \rightarrow X$
INY	Increment Y register	$Y + 1 \rightarrow Y$
JMP	Jump unconditional	Jump to location M
JSR	Jump to subroutine	Jump to subroutine at location M
LDA	Load Accumulator	$M \rightarrow A$
LDX	Load X register	$M \rightarrow X$
LDY	Load Y register	$M \rightarrow Y$
LSR	Logical shift right	$0 \rightarrow \boxed{} \rightarrow C$

NOP	No operation	Increment Program Counter
ORA	Logical OR	$A \lor M \to A$
PHA	Push Acc on stack	$A \to S; \ SP-1 \to SP$
PHP	Push PSR on stack	$PSR \to S; \ SP-1 \to SP$
PLA	Pull Acc from stack	$SP+1 \to SP; \ S \to A$
PLP	Pull PSR from stack	$SP+1 \to SP; \ S \to PSR$
ROL	Rotate left	$\leftarrow \boxed{} \leftarrow C \rfloor$
ROR	Rotate right	$\lfloor C \rfloor \boxed{} \to \rfloor$
RTI	Return from interrupt	Return to next location from interrupt
RTS	Return from subroutine	Return to next location from call
SBC	Subtract with carry	$A-M-C \to A$
SEC	Set carry	$1 \to C$
SED	Set decimal mode	$1 \to D$
SEI	Set interrupt inhibit	$1 \to I$
STA	Store accumulator	$A \to M$
STX	Store X register	$X \to M$
STY	Store Y register	$Y \to M$
TAX	Transfer Accum to X register	$A \to X$
TAY	Transfer Accum to Y register	$A \to Y$
TSX	Transfer PSR to X register	$PSR \to X$
TXA	Transfer X register to Accum	$X \to A$
TXS	Transfer X register to PSR	$X \to PSR$
TYA	Transfer Y register to Accum	$Y \to A$

Operational symbolism abbreviations

A	. . . Accumulator	
X	. . . Index register X	
Y	. . . Index register Y	
PSR	. . . Program status register	
SP	. . . Stack pointer	
S	. . . Location corresponding to SP	
N	. . . N bit in PSR	
I	. . . I bit in PSR	
Z	. . . Z bit in PSR	
D	. . . D bit in PSR	
C	. . . C bit in PSR	
V	. . . V bit in PSR	The arrow $\to$, means 'where the result
$\land$	. . . Logical AND	is placed'
$\veebar$	. . . Logical Exclusive OR	M means memory or, in the case of
$\lor$	. . . Logical OR	immediate mode, a number.

147

Operations between memory and accumulator

	IMM		Z PGE		ABS		Z PGE, X		ABS, X		ABS, Y		INDX INDR		INDR INDX		PSR bits
LDA	A9		A5		AD		B5		BD		B9		A1		B1		NZ
	1	2	1	3	2	4	1	4	2	4	2	4	1	6	1	5	
STA	No code!		85		8D		95		9D		99		81		91		/
			1	3	2	4	1	4	2	5	2	5	1	6	1	6	
ADC	69		65		6D		75		7D		79		61		71		NZCV
	1	2	1	3	2	4	1	4	2	4	2	4	1	6	1	5	
SBC	E9		E5		ED		F5		FD		F9		E1		F1		NZCV
	1	2	1	3	2	4	1	4	2	4	2	4	1	6	1	5	
CMP	C9		C5		CD		D5		DD		D9		C1		D1		NZC
	1	2	1	3	2	4	1	4	2	4	2	4	1	6	1	5	
AND	29		25		2D		35		3D		39		21		31		NZ
	1	2	1	3	2	4	1	4	2	4	2	4	1	6	1	5	
ORA	O9		O5		OD		15		1D		19		O1		11		NZ
	1	2	1	3	2	4	1	4	2	4	2	4	1	6	1	5	
EOR	49		45		4D		55		5D		59		41		51		NZ
	1	2	1	3	2	4	1	4	2	4	2	4	1	6	1	5	

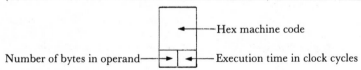

Hex machine code

Number of bytes in operand ——→ ← —— Execution time in clock cycles

Register to register transfers and counting

	Implied
TAX	AA
TXA	8A
TXS	9A
TSX	BA
TAY	A8

1. No operands required

2. All take two clock cycles

3. All update N and Z bits except TXS

	Implied
TYA	98
INX	E8
DEX	CA
INY	C8
DEY	88

Single bit operations on processor status register

CLC	18
SEC	38
CLD	D8
SED	F8

1. No operands required

2. All take two clock cycles

3. Action on PSR bits as title indicates

CLV	B8
CLI	58
SEI	78

Operations between memory and index registers

	Imm		Z PGE		ABS		Z PGE, Y		ABS, Y		Z PGE, X		ABS, X		PSR bits
LDX	A2		A6		AE		B6		BE		No code		No code		NZ
	1	2	1	3	2	4	1	4	2	4					
STX	No code		86		8E		96		No code		No code		No code		/
			1	3	2	4	1	4							
LDY	A0		A4		AC		No code		No code		B4		BC		NZ
	1	2	1	3	2	4					1	4	2	4	
STY	No code		84		8C		No code		No code		94		No code		
			1	3	2	4					1	4			
CPX	E0		E4		EC		No code		No code		No code		No code		NZC
	1	2	1	3	2	4									
CPY	C0		C4		CC		No code		No code		No code		No code		NZC
	1	2	1	3	2	4									

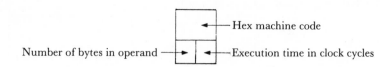

Number of bytes in operand ⟶ | | ⟵ Hex machine code / ⟵ Execution time in clock cycles

150

Conditional branches

	Relative
BNE	D0
BEQ	F0
BPL	10
BCC	90

1. No action on PSR bits
2. Forward branches have positive operands. Backward branches have negative operands
3. All have single byte operands
4. All take 2 clock cycles

	Relative
BMI	30
BVC	50
BVS	70
BCS	B0

Unconditional jumps

	ABS		*Indirect*	
JMP	4C		6C	
	2	3	2	5
JSR	20		No code	
	2	6		

No action on PSR bits

Break and returns

	Implied
BRK	00
RTS	60
RTI	40

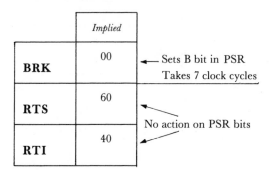

⟵ Sets B bit in PSR
Takes 7 clock cycles

No action on PSR bits

Shift and rotate operations

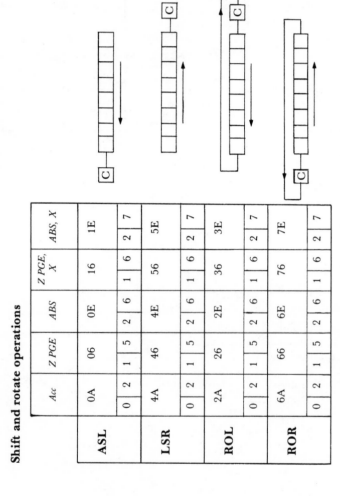

	Acc	Z PGE	ABS	Z PGE, X	ABS, X
ASL	0A	06	0E	16	1E
	0 2	1 5	2 6	1 6	2 7
LSR	4A	46	4E	56	5E
	0 2	1 5	2 6	1 6	2 7
ROL	2A	26	2E	36	3E
	0 2	1 5	2 6	1 6	2 7
ROR	6A	66	6E	76	7E
	0 2	1 5	2 6	1 6	2 7

All update the N Z and C bits except that LSR always resets the N bit to '0'

Incrementing, decrementing memory and bit test

	Z PGE		ABS		Z PGE, X		ABS, X	
INC	E6		EE		F6		FE	
	1	5	2	6	1	6	2	7
DEC	C6		CE		D6		DE	
	1	5	2	6	1	6	2	7
BIT	24		2C		No code		No code	
	1	3	2	4				

Stack operations

	Implied		
PHA	48		No action on PSR bits
	0	3	
PLA	68		Updates N and Z bits
	0	4	
PHP	08		No action on PSR bits
	0	3	
PLP	28		No action on PSR bits
	0	4	

Appendix 2

Useful conversion tables

Powers of 2

$2^0 = 1$	$2^4 = 16$	$2^8 = 256$	$2^{12} = 4096$
$2^1 = 2$	$2^5 = 32$	$2^9 = 512$	$2^{13} = 8192$
$2^2 = 4$	$2^6 = 64$	$2^{10} = 1024$	$2^{14} = 16024$
$2^3 = 8$	$2^7 = 128$	$2^{11} = 2048$	$2^{15} = 32048$

Hex/decimal/ASCII conversion

ASCII character	0	1	2	3	4	5	6	7	8	9	space	
Hex	30	31	32	33	34	35	36	37	38	39	20	
Decimal	48	49	50	51	52	53	54	55	56	57	32	

ASCII character	A	B	C	D	E	F	G	H	I	J	K	L	M
Hex	41	42	43	44	45	46	47	48	49	4A	4B	4C	4D
Decimal	65	66	67	68	69	70	71	72	73	74	75	76	77

ASCII character	N	O	P	Q	R	S	T	U	V	W	X	Y	Z
Hex	4E	4F	50	51	52	53	54	55	56	57	58	59	5A
Decimal	78	79	80	81	82	83	84	85	86	87	88	89	90

Table of odds and ends

```
        4 bits = 1 nibble
    2 nibbles = 1 byte
     2 bytes = an absolute address
     1 page = 256 bytes
     4 pages = 1K
        64K = 256 pages
     Page 0 = 0000 to 00FF hex
     7F hex = + 127 dec = largest positive number in two's complement
     80 hex = —128 dec = largest negative number in two's
              complement
     FF hex = 225 dec = largest number in unsigned binary
```

Index